Alternative Careers
For Teachers

Alternative Careers for Teachers
Revised Edition

Sandy Pollack

THE HARVARD COMMON PRESS
Harvard and Boston, Massachusetts

The Harvard Common Press
535 Albany Street
Boston, Massachusetts 02118

Printed in the United States of America.

Library of Congress Cataloging in Publication Data

Pollack, Sandra.
    Alternative careers for teachers.

    Bibliography: p.
    Includes index.
    1. Teaching—Vocational guidance—United States.
2. Occupational mobility—United States. 3. Teachers
college graduates—Employment—United States.
4. Professions—United States. I. Title.
LB1775.P6 1984   371.1'0023   84-19727
ISBN 0-916782-61-1
ISBN 0-916782-60-3 (pbk.)

Cover design by Peter Good

10 9 8 7 6 5 4

To my husband, Herb, who imbued me with the spirit of an entrepreneur and who encouraged me to launch my own alternative career.

Contents

Preface ix

Introduction xi

1. Why Do Teachers Need Alternatives? 1

2. Trainer: A New Title For Teachers 9

3. The World of Computers 15

4. Careers in Personnel 26

5. Creative Careers 31

6. Educational and Nonprofit Organizations 42

7. Sales Careers 50

8. Self-Employment 57

9. Working for the Government 67

10. Alternative Careers: More Options to Consider 76

11. How to Get a Job If You Really Want to Teach 91

12. Looking Ahead to 1990: The Best Careers 99

13. Making It Happen 103

Appendix 139

Bibliography 143

Index 154

Acknowledgements

Much has changed for me since the first printing in 1979 of *Alternative Careers for Teachers*. After having influenced and assisted many former teachers with their own transitions into the business world, I myself replaced years of teaching and administration with an alternative career. In 1981 I formed my own executive search and placement agency, Sandy Pollack Associates Inc., a testimony to the question "Is there life after teaching?"

It is impossible to acknowledge everyone who contributes to the writing of a book. A complete list would have to include all the people who have had an impact upon my life. In this vein, I want to thank my father, who treated me as an equal before the inception of the Women's Liberation Movement and who, interestingly enough, was an entrepreneur, as I have become.

In my second career it has been my husband, Herb, president of his own electronics company, who has been my mentor. I admired his business acumen and absorbed more of his philosophy than I realized. When I formed my own corporation, his sage advice and support helped me through my early trials and errors. Since he is in the electronics business—the same industry I serve—he was one of my first clients!

Other friends in business have become clients, too. I am thankful for the confidence they placed in me to choose qualified professionals to work in their companies. Warm thanks to Elizabeth Oppenhimer who helped me to set the tone for the job descriptions in the field of advertising.

A major editing of the manuscript was done by Dorothy Seymour. Her attention to the finest detail was commendable.

To Therese York, my secretary, I owe more than "thank you." Without her dedication to the company, it would not be easy to accomplish all the goals I set, including the typing of this manuscript—an extra-curricular project.

To Kathleen Cushman, the executive editor of The Harvard Common Press, who believed in the value of this book, I owe thanks for bestowing on me the title *author*, which had always been one of my life's goals.

Sandy Pollack
Lexington, Massachusetts
June, 1984

Preface

Living in a school environment in which almost everyone is a teacher tends to give you a narrow perspective on the rest of the working world. In no other profession do all your peers engage in almost the same activity as you. In other professions, job changing is a more common occurrence, places where upward mobility can precipitate career changes several times during the course of a lifetime. Twenty percent of all employees change jobs each year, and grow accustomed to the process.

For teachers, however, who may never have changed jobs in their lives, the question, "Is there life after teaching?" is asked with sobriety and urgency. A change of profession seems like an impossible hurdle to leap.

But it doesn't have to be.

After all, you were not born a teacher, were you? You chose it, for whatever reasons. You can switch gears at any time and choose from an entire gamut of new careers, ones you may never have considered at an earlier age.

You are not facing the end of your life. You are probably

facing an intriguing beginning. Unlike a novice, however, you are bringing a wealth of knowledge and experience with you. You will find that your most valuable assets are your bachelor's or master's degrees—the door opening on the world.

In this book you will find numerous success stories of former teachers who have entered new professions. Success stories abound. Look around, and you, too, will make your own discoveries.

Know what you want, know where to look, and then, as the coach says in sports: Go out and give 'em hell!

Introduction

When I wrote the first edition of this book in 1978, there was an oversupply of teachers, and thousands of graduates were unable to find jobs in their chosen field. Experienced teachers, many who loved teaching, were shocked to find themselves trapped in the statistics of the newly "riffed."

At that time, while working at Middlesex Community College and cognizant of declining enrollments and their statistical ramifications, I developed a workshop entitled, "Alternative Careers for Teachers," the material from which this book emerged.

Angry and depressed because their supposedly stable careers had vanished (or would soon vanish), teachers flocked to the workshop for career information, but it soon became clear that some were motivated by more than "riffing"; they wanted a change in profession.

What were their reasons for seeking a change?

For many teachers, the fun had disappeared from teaching. In many school districts the ability to teach without disciplining was only a Utopian dream. In addition, many teachers were burned out, as it's called, from trying to motivate passive children brought up on television who were used to being entertained.

Why are teachers still seeking change in 1984? One of the reasons is the attack to which our schools and teachers have been exposed.

In 1983 the government authorized several studies on the status of education in America. One of the reports denigrated both schools and teachers by concluding that there existed a "rising tide of mediocrity" in our schools. This blow was struck by the National Commission on Excellence in Education.

In 1984, in an attempt to effect educational reform, Senator Paul Tsongas of Massachusetts polled his constituents with the following results: 93.1 percent agreed that the quality of education was on the decline. In this sampling of 47,000 people there were many parents, of course. How can teachers feel good about their profession when they are held in low esteem by so many people?

National standardized test scores, too, have proven that students are not learning adequately. Teachers have taken the brunt of everyone's anger. No one is ready to admit that a child is affected by a changed society: millions of students come to school hungry, many are victims of unhappy homes or are latch-key children without daytime guidance or moral support—conditions that affect their ability to learn. Schools can only reflect society and cannot be a panacea for society's flaws, despite government and community protests to the contrary. Nevertheless, teachers are blamed for the lowered test scores.

Pressure placed on administrators to improve academic performance is passed on to the teachers, thus heating up the atmosphere in schools. Teachers already burdened with larger classes and heavier teaching schedules resent the accusations and additional pressure; burnout is an evident professional hazard. Further demoralization is felt when low salary increments are begrudgingly granted after acrimonious political battles between union and school negotiatiors; teachers see this action as a sign of their low value in society. Beset by financial concerns, too, teachers initially listen only half-heartedly to peers who have found jobs in industry, but they listen more seriously when they hear that their friends' salaries have doubled in two or three years;

then they, too, begin to make inquiries into the alternatives. (An experienced teacher's salary is $20,000, the *starting* salary in industry.)

Proof that the profession is not as prized as it was previously is a 1981 poll that drew the conclusion that only 22 percent of teachers would choose the profession again.

In some cases, even when teachers have been happy they may not have a choice, because certain demographic areas are still experiencing layoffs. In fact, there is expected to be a 33 percent layoff of high school teachers in the eighties.

Many teachers leave urban schools because they have been the victims of crime and physical attacks. The report entitled *Chaos in the Classroom: Enemy of American Education* (retitled *Disorder in Our Schools* because of the backlash) contains shocking statistics on crimes perpetrated each month against teachers and students, some of which are enumerated below.

- 3,000,000 schoolchildren are victims of crime, mostly stealing
- 6,000 teachers are robbed each month
- 125,000 teachers are threatened with physical harm
- 250,000 students suffer physical attacks
- 1,000 teachers require medical care

How long would you last in an urban school?

Despite the fact that teachers are seeking their futures outside the school system (you will find more reasons in Chapter 1) and despite the lack of opportunity in some parts of the country, the newspapers produce glaring headlines predicting an imminent baby boom. Yes, there is an increase in births at present, but the recent increase in the birth rate as career women begin to have their families will not create another boom. The impact of the women's movement, the divorce rate, the increasing number of working women, the cost of child rearing, and the ever-increasing bite of inflation are all working against such a possibility.

There is, however, a projected increase in the school population expected to start in 1985 and to reach a peak in 1990, an increase that may create a shortage of teachers.

What will the reaction on future teachers be to the criticism of our schools? After all, we do need new teachers each year to replace the teachers who leave the system. What is being done to improve the quality of education?

The United States Department of Education has been sending panels of volunteer educators across the country in an effort to locate and publicize the best high schools. The Ford Foundation, too, recently awarded $20,000 grants to 100 superior schools in 47 cities. Articles are springing up in education journals analyzing the characteristics of the best schools, in an attempt, perhaps, to counter adverse publicity caused by the release of critical government reports. Ironically, in these reports not one classroom teacher's voice is heard—further testimony that teachers' opinions were not valued.

Fortunately, school systems are beginning to respond to critics by instituting educational reforms like merit bonuses and raising the academic standard for students and teachers. Some of these issues, however, are highly controversial and are opposed by teachers themselves. Although reform is being discussed, it still remains to be seen whether a country that has voted for Propositions Thirteen and two-and-a-half is going to pay for the new programs. If we are to attract the best-qualified candidates, changes and incentives will have to be initiated. Even now there is a shortage of math and science teachers, and there will be somewhat greater demand, too, for language teachers because of the back-to-basics movement that is growing in the country's schools from elementary to college level.

Nevertheless, six percent of all teachers will leave the teaching field every year, for one reason or another, and will want to seek alternatives.

Observation and analysis of publications concerning employment trends indicates that we are educating more people for whom there will be fewer suitable and satisfying professional jobs. The liberal arts graduate (the category into which most teachers fall) may be unqualified to compete for the jobs of the future. Teachers in particular, therefore, will have to assess their abilities in order to translate them into marketable skills, many of them technical, outside the teaching field.

It is becoming increasingly clear that training in finance, computers, and other technical fields is of major importance in today's job market. Teachers are not exempt from this need. In fact, they might benefit from such training more than any other group, especially when seeking administrative positions and higher incomes. For teachers, lack of computer and technical training will mean frustration and immobility in making a career change and the necessity of accepting a lower salary in a new field; for the new graduate, there will be fewer career opportunities. That is why a thorough knowledge of career options and techniques, many of which are explained in this book, is essential.

Most teachers have never considered any profession other than teaching. My experience with hundreds of teachers of all ages who have previously participated in my classes and workshops tells me that they need assistance in both recognizing their talents and applying them to different professions.

This book is an attempt to educate teachers about themselves—their skills, their qualifications, and their potential in the job market. For teachers do have skills, above and beyond their ability to teach math, French, or home economics to sixth graders. It is a common but crucial mistake for teachers to underestimate their abilities outside the four walls of a schoolroom.

This book will attempt to describe diverse professions that use the far-reaching talents of teachers. Teachers can be found in industry, in social service agencies, in nonprofit organizations, and in businesses, often their own. I have personally placed teachers in all these fields, where they are happy and contented—proof that there is "life beyond the classroom."

In my workshops for teachers there has been ample need demonstrated for a how-to segment. The last chapter of this book, the how-to section, stresses the practical aspects of the teacher's job hunt: how to identify skills, how to gather career information, how to conduct an interview, and how to execute a successful job hunting campaign, from the early gathering of data to the negotiation of salary.

The college graduate or the re-entry adult seeking a career in teaching will find a chapter devoted to specific techniques that have brought success to others.

For teachers, ex-teachers, graduates, and career changers who know how to prepare, how to proceed, and how to follow through, there is a myriad of alternatives on the horizon.

1. Why Do Teachers Need Alternatives?

Our world is changing so rapidly—from robots working alongside employees to astronauts repairing satellites in space—that, to some teachers, sitting in a classroom teaching a group of children how to read the words *house* and *chair* has begun to seem limiting. They want to leave what they perceive as the narrow world of teaching and seek their fortunes in the "adult world." After six or seven years of work with children, they feel that they are no longer the same people they were when they entered the profession. "We have grown up," they say. "Our goals and values have changed."

Previously, the world of business was disparaged by teachers because of the perception that business practices were not as lofty as teaching. That concept has changed, and the word *business* has lost its negative connotation. Teachers are not, after all, excluded from inflation or from our society's interest in comfort and luxuries—luxuries they feel business will pay for, in the form of higher salaries.

Re-entry teachers, too, who have spent years bringing up their

1

own children and who have not worked recently are seeking options outside the classroom; the business and industrial world appears to be a viable alternative for them as well.

Victims of cutbacks, graduates, and retired teachers are joining the quest for alternatives. Others—dedicated teachers—want to have knowledge "just in case!" Counselors, college professors, and librarians need to have knowledge to present to experienced teachers, novices, and students.

From talking with teachers, it is clear to me that they are ready for a change. They are ready for a challenge and the stimulation a new career can bring. They are ready to compete and to be rewarded. They are ready to join their peers who have already made successful transitions. They are ready to be part of the fast-moving world of robots and computers that appears to be leaving them behind. They are ready to accept the risks and rewards of launching "a business of my own" that fits their present needs more closely. They are ready to seek new opportunities in the social services, too.

In the workshops I conducted, teachers candidly shared with the group their reasons for ferreting out the alternatives, some of which are quoted below. As you read, you may find yourself nodding in agreement, since teachers share a commonality of experiences and concerns, as you know. Many other feelings were expressed as well, some which are not mentioned here, so be assured: whatever your sentiment and motivation, you are not alone.

The Teacher Who's Ready to Move On

"Don't misunderstand me. These eight years have been very satisfying. I truly enjoy teaching science. But I've already done it. I know that I can accomplish more. I've enrolled in a graduate MBA program. It's time to take a risk."

This teacher was leaving his school system in order to pursue a career in an entirely new field. In the book *Changing Careers After Thirty-Five*, published in 1971, Professor Dale I. Hiestand of Columbia University discusses a different type of dropout: the educated adult who drops out of one career and enters a graduate program in an entirely new field, a field that accommodates a changed set of values and an altered view of personal talents and attributes. You, too, may have decided that your view of yourself has changed and that you want to change professions. Why not? I have interviewed teachers who are studying the law, studying for nursing careers, studying public relations, and so on. Why not you, too?

The Teacher Who Finds Teaching a Dead End

"I'm single and self-supporting. Most of my friends are teachers. I love my fellow teachers dearly, but teaching is a social dead end for me. I want to meet professionals in other fields. And I want more professional advancement that I can get here."

Within the hierarchy of the school system there is limited opportunity for upward mobility and diversity. The business world is seen as a ladder to a more varied professional and social life.

The Battered Teacher

"When I was attacked by a student who was unhappy with the disciplinary action I was forced to take against him, he slashed me with a knife. That was two months ago. Every day that I come to work I am in fear. Three days ago one of the students in the school—not one of my students—walked up to me and used me as a punching bag. I'm not sure whether it was meant for me or not. I didn't report it. What's the use? He might take out more of his anger against me. I've had it with teaching." (See the Introduction for actual statistics on school incidents of violence.)

The Soon-to-be-Retired Teacher

"Just because I'm retiring, it doesn't mean that I don't have fifteen productive years ahead of me—maybe more! Right now, I do feel drained—kids can do that to you —and I admit that I've put a great deal of my creative energies into this job. But after a few weeks of vacation in the sun, I know that I'll be looking around for either a business of my own or . . . . What do you have in mind for me?"

The Teacher Who Can't Afford to Teach

"I wouldn't be seeking an alternative career if I didn't need to earn more money. I just cannot afford to buy any item that is not an absolute necessity. Vacations are out of the question. Is there a place where I can earn five thousand dollars more than I'm making now?"

This teacher had been teaching for two years in a very small suburban town. I was able to help him find a technical writing position that paid him seven thousand dollars more than he was earning and included the reality of very rapid increases. Unlike the education field, industry pays between seven and twelve percent in annual salary increases, and more if you become a manager or change jobs. Teachers are not exempt from the need for greater financial security or the desire for a higher level of living.

The Recent Graduate Who Decides Not to Teach

"I had no idea what it was going to be like teaching in that class-room. It was like a zoo. They threw spitballs and airplanes at me—one dunce even stole my lunch. I'll never go back."

Even though students are preparing for a school teaching job, the reality of disciplining and controlling students may be beyond their abilities or at odds with their expectations; in fact, twenty-three percent fail to enter the teaching profession. These teachers, nevertheless, are unprepared for another career and are seeking information about alternatives.

Other graduates simply can't find teaching jobs. Chapter 11 is devoted to graduates and re-entry teachers who need help in conducting a more thorough search to uncover a teaching job.

The Insecure Teacher

"All around me, I hear the muffled cries of my friends who have been 'excessed.' One of my friends was laid off three times from three different schools because of enrollment drops. Now she's unemployed.

"I love teaching, but I can't live like this waiting for the ax to fall. I must know now. What else is there?"

This book describes career paths that answer the question "What else is there?"—paths many teachers have already followed successfully. Before they took the big step into business or another profession, however, they asked question after question in their attempt to probe the outer surface of a world that held many unknowns.

The following questions, actually asked by teachers, may contain several you have pondered, too.

Questions Teachers Ask.

1. "How do vacations in the business world compare with teaching vacations?"

2. "What is a job description?"

3. "Do I have to go back to school?"

4. "Are teachers overqualified or underqualified for certain jobs?"

5. "I need a good salary. Can I afford to quit teaching?"

6. "Suppose I don't want to work in the business world? What then?"

7. "How do I know what I can do besides teach?"

8. "Are there jobs elsewhere that end at three o'clock, as my teaching job does?"

These questions indicate naivete concerning the so-called real working world. Teachers often state that the most fundamental aspects of business and industry are alien to them. If you feel this way, too, don't be surprised. Most people don't know very much concerning professions outside of their own. To set you on the right track and start the demystification process, let's answer the questions above.

Answers to Questions Teachers Ask.

1. Colleges, hospitals, and social service agencies usually provide four weeks of paid vacation time. Business offers two weeks plus an average of ten paid holidays a year and very liberal sick time. (If you're counting, that's three and a half weeks right there.) Most companies also permit time off to attend conferences and even time to present talks or lectures. Business is much more flexible and human than people think. (Haven't you seen businesspeople enjoying themselves over their two-hour lunches?)

2. A job description details the duties, skills, educational requirements, and salary of a particular job within the organization. Most large companies have job analysts who write these descriptions. (See Chapter 9 for a Peace Corps job description.)

Within companies, job descriptions are placed on bulletin boards to announce new openings in different departments; since most openings are filled internally, it is important for you to get into the system yourself!

3. Most jobs mentioned in this book require no additional degrees. (After all, fifty percent of teachers already hold master's degrees and doctorates—a tribute to their professionalism; these degrees may be applicable.) Business and social service agencies require relevant training, however, so a specific course of action may be necessary when you have made up your mind. If you choose medicine, law, or a similar specialty, you will definitely need another degree.

Although a Master of Business Administration is not a panacea (there could easily be a glut of M.B.A.s because there were 55,000 graduates in 1983), many executives think that this is the route to the top. My personal feeling is that if you are successful in obtaining a position with a company, let it pay for your degree, if you want one. To be honest, however, I must say that former teachers have had success in entering industry at higher salaries than they had been earning after taking their M.B.A.s in finance or marketing—two very desirable areas today. You can see that there are no easy answers when it comes to your own particular case.

4. You are never overqualified for a job you want to do. If you are certain you want a particular job, let's say that of a word processor, then it is up to you to convince the interviewer that you are not overqualified and that you're going to stay on the job. When you say to the interviewer, "I'm just using this job as a steppingstone to the next one," the interviewer will think that you'll be leaving the company in the lurch as soon as you find a better opportunity; the company would prefer to avoid such a situation. Always interview for a job as though it is the only one for you; after all, it is, at the time. If you are using the job as a

steppingstone, keep that to yourself; an interview is not a confessional.

For certain positions that need proven specific skills, you will be underqualified. Isn't everyone unqualified for many positions? If a company has a thousand employees and you answer an ad for a personnel manager, you would be underqualified; but if it is a small company, you could qualify after taking a few relevant seminars or courses in personnel. Again, if you are confident, it will be easier to be convincing.

5. Never quit *any* job before you have another. Of course there are jobs that pay more than teaching. Higher-paying jobs are found in computer programming, technical writing, sales, law, management, personnel, training, and your own business, to name only a few possibilities. But let me repeat: Never quit any job until you have a job offer firmly in hand; the results could be disastrous in terms of lost time and money! The average length of time it takes to find a job is six months, especially for career changers. Naturally, if you have an adequate (one-year) financial cushion, you can quit your job and even take a trip to Tahiti.

6. If you choose not to work in the business world, that decision should be based on informed research. There are many business situations that fit teachers, like being an administrator in a nursery school (such as Kinder-Care) or becoming a travel agent, or being an independent bookseller to schools; these are all business world occupations. (This book has many other suggestions.) If you have truly decided that business is unsuited to your needs, then you can look into the social service world, government, college administration, nonprofit associations, and agencies like the Red Cross or the YWCA. But you must not delude yourself: all agencies function with budgets and so act similarly to businesses; the bottom line places restraints on all institutions and forces them to be prudent with their budgets—not entirely unlike their business neighbors.

7. This book is filled with suggestions. As you read, make a list of those jobs that appeal to you and find out more about the requirements, parameters, and merits of each position.

8. If you take on a selling job, you may be able to end your day at three o'clock, but of course, you will not be as successful as you would if you spent a full business day on the job. Selling books and insurance to teachers and other school personnel can also end at three, but may require appointments at night, too. You may be able to make a special arrangement with an ad agency, a bank, or a social service agency. In almost all cases, full-time jobs require that you work from 8:30 A.M. to 5:30 P.M. or from 9:00 A.M. to 5 P.M., depending on the company; business usually works on a nine-hour day: eight hours of work and an hour or a half hour for lunch. I have, however, included in my discussion many jobs that are of a part-time nature because part-time employment has become very desirable, especially for women who are bringing up families and want to devote less than full time to their careers.

Now that we have laid the fantasies to rest, it is time to start replacing them with realities. Even if you decide to stay in teaching, you will be a much better-informed teacher.

In this book you will find career information and a set of tools that will permit you to explore the unfamiliar world that lies outside the somewhat protected boundaries of your profession. Don't permit fear of the unknown or fear of failure to stop you from flying. A new career can serve as the catalyst to a rekindled professional life, one that can attain surprising heights (see my own story in Chapter 8). Margaret Mead has written that humans use only ten percent of their potential in a lifetime, so your world contains a vast oyster with a pearl waiting to be discovered.

Go for it!

2. Trainer: A New Title For Teachers

If you want to teach and haven't heard about the training field, you are in for a pleasant surprise.

Today's employers have accepted the responsibility for their employees' well-being, both professionally and personally. In order to stay competitive with one another and attract the best employees, almost all companies have had to offer attractive benefits. As you can imagine, taking care of employees' needs, especially in giant corporations, is no easy task.

In order to accomplish their lofty, paternalistic goals of creating a working environment conducive to their employees' growth, strange as it may seem to educators who are unaware of business practices, companies have entered the business of education.

Here is where the teacher-trainer enters the scene.

Types of Training

Almost all institutions and companies in the country hire employees with diverse educational, cultural, and racial back-

9

grounds. During the course of their employment, an employee may need an additional skill, such as English (for the foreign born); or French (for the manager who is going to a foreign plant); accounting, computer operations, career development—any number of other subjects varying from "How to Read Blueprints" to "How to Recognize and Manage Stress." Don't think that you cannot be a trainer because you can't tell a blueprint from a blue-fish; you can hire a consultant to teach the course, because as a trainer, you will be given a budget that can be used as you see fit.

Most trainers do a combination of planning, scheduling, hiring of special consultants, and training in specialties they have themselves developed over a period of time. (Let's face it, if you see a workshop conducted twice, you can probably teach it the next time.) Trainers also rent or buy a varied supply of films and other kinds of packaged programs from media manufacturers. You can see that training has become a big business. In fact, to fill the need to disseminate training information, training magazines and newspapers have sprung up. (See *Management, Training,* or *Careers* in the bibliography.)

Workshops and courses are conducted on an ongoing basis almost every day of the week in large companies. And where are these classes held? Right on the premises! Some companies have even built elaborate training rooms with the latest media equipment. If the company hasn't a large enough facility, classes may be held in the cafeteria. Often (usually for management or sales training) the company rents room at convention centers or hotels. Digital Equipment Corporation, the giant mini-computer company, has helicopters that transport employees back and forth from the plant where they work to another facility where their training classes are held. I was impressed and amused when a helicopter came in for a landing in the parking lot where I was standing (I could almost hear my grandmother say, "Only in America").

"And who," you may ask, "is doing the teaching of all these classes?"

Those of you who have never heard of the training field will be surprised to learn that many trainers are former schoolteachers.

Working with motivated adults in an environment free of discipline problems may be the nearest thing to Utopia for someone who loves to teach. I myself have taught at the elementary, junior high, and senior high levels, and each level has held its unique pleasures for me, but no teaching experience has been as stimulating and gratifying as a former position in which I taught adults on the college level and trained adults in industry.

Of course, types of training vary with the company's needs and objectives and the commitment of its management. Some companies have joined hands with the Adult Educators Association in promulgating a goal of lifelong learning. Polaroid, one of the most committed companies, runs a 24-hour-a-day school in which its 10,400 employees on any of three shifts can select from more than a hundred courses and programs. Employees can choose from

- Spoken English I, II
- Assertiveness Skills
- High School Physics
- Math Development
- German, Spanish, Portuguese, French, Dutch
- Reading and Writing Skills
- Coping with Stress
- Introduction to Personal Computers
- Study Skills
- Math Review Lab
- Personnel Policy

and an entire gamut of engineering and management courses.

All the above may be taught in addition to on-the-job training, which takes place in most departments of all companies. Teachers are hired for all these subjects as well as for administrative roles, counseling, curriculum development, and a variety of media activities. One company has even hired teachers to instruct its newly-hired technicians in what is called proper professional attire. Supervisory and management training is ongoing in most companies. Many teachers have learned how to train employees in an assembly-line skill, even though they had never seen an assembly line before.

Several large companies like GTE Sylvania, ITT, and Arthur D. Little contract to train foreign students—both at private universities like Massachusetts Institute of Technology and in the institutes that have been founded in their own plants. In-house industrial schools are a growing trend. Companies also hire counselors to assist foreign students in solving any problems that may arise during the time they live in the United States. One student, for example, wanted to get married without his parents' approval. The counselor not only discouraged it but even managed to prevent it. I have launched several elementary teachers into these jobs, which have been instrumental in introducing them into an international climate they never could have envisioned and which were used as steppingstones to management positions. One former teacher now earns $40,000 as a Director of Human Resources.

From time to time special needs develop among the students, so tutors, special teachers, curriculum developers, and teachers with a linguistic background are hired to cater to these needs.

In order to find the above situations, you should read technical journals like *Electronic News,* business newspapers like the *Wall Street Journal,* or other periodicals in which announcements are made of contracts and awards. A large new contract may indicate a need for additional staff.

Some companies have established training centers away from the regular plant where employees can be trained. The telephone company has one of the most sophisticated centers of all. One beautiful facility at Marlboro, Massachusetts, provides sleeping and dining quarters for employees who need extensive training. This center employs librarians, photographers, media experts, and writers; it houses an entire print shop, too.

In addition to all the above, industry hires psychologists, lawyers, artists, and retirement specialists. After all, employees spend much of their lives on the job and bring with them such personal problems as alcoholism, divorce, illness, stress, and death in the family. Responsible companies respond to these needs.

The idea of training is not new. The concept originated with the United States government about forty years ago. During World War II, the necessity of training large numbers of military personnel was the inspiration for a new system. Anyone involved in these programs remembers the intensity of the training and the efficiency of the programs. To this day the government retains a huge staff of trainers who work in some of the fields previously outlined. (The chapter on government discusses other programs as well.) The important fact to remember is that training is ubiquitous, and teachers are hired to do the training because of their unique skills and experience.

How to Break into the Field

There are several national training organizations. One of the best is the American Society for Training and Development (see Appendix). The educational background of ASTD members ranges from B.A.'s to Ph.D's and runs the full gamut of teaching disciplines. The value of joining organizations is discussed in Chapter 13; I cannot overemphasize the importance of membership and participation. Attend meetings and conferences where you will see techniques demonstrated, trainers in action, and workshops come alive.

How can you find out more about this work in order to stimulate your interest and prepare you for this field? Take the following steps:

1. Look for a branch of ASTD in your area and join or attend a meeting.

2. Plan on attending one of its excellent workshops where techniques as well as materials are shared; these handouts are invaluable towards starting you on your own career.

3. Talk to the members: How did they get started? What specialty have workshop leaders perfected? Was it career development for employees? Supervisory training? Affirmative Action? Sales training? English? Determine the specialty in which you have the greatest interest. Attend several workshops. Read every book in the field. (I started with Assertiveness Training and Career Development.)

4. After reading all the information you can find, write your own workshop.

5. Give a workshop at a local continuing education division of a college, or at a Y. Revise the material and teach it again.

6. Become a consultant in one of these subjects.

7. How can you become a consultant? Make out a simple flier. Enclose it with a letter to a hundred companies. Follow up on your flier with a phone call and a visit.

8. Present a workshop at an ASTD meeting. You will be surprised at the business you will get and the people who will get to know you.

If all this sounds like pie in the sky, let me assure you that it is not. Many people began this way, as consultants, and are now in great demand. Others have used this consulting route to land full-time training positions. Many have expanded their consulting into large businesses. One of the reasons I started my own employment agency was the contacts I had made as a trainer in industry; these contacts were very helpful in getting me started. Today we call contacts *networking*.

To apply for training positions, try colleges, banks, nonprofit companies, and small companies; all of these are more inclined to hire former teachers with no formal training experience than are the large companies. Be bold. Don't expect the door to open just because you knocked. Be resourceful and forceful; make it open.

Affirmative Action programs and the ongoing needs of organizations has caused a proliferation of career opportunity in this exciting field. Seek out this creative, viable alternative where salaries start at $20,000 or $25,000.

Training is teaching at its best.

3. The World Of Computers

You don't have to own an Apple Computer or observe a ten-year-old computer wizard to know that we live in the age of the computer.

The computer industry's growth is so explosive—a hundred percent increase every year compared with an average of twenty-five percent for other industries—and career opportunities so varied and vast that you can hardly be indifferent to the world of computers. Even if you think that the only form of communication is face-to-face platform teaching, let me urge you to explore the possibilities within this burgeoning industry. Don't think that the industry is limited to just programming. Thousands of teachers have made successful transitions as technical writers, trainers, salespeople, curriculum developers, coordinators, and so forth (discussed in this chapter), and many have been promoted, after a few years, to supervisors and managers, or have started their own businesses. Not one of those I interviewed would return to teaching, a previously loved profession.

Even if you decide not to seek a career in computers, you

should become computer-literate (aware of what computers do and how they do it, and of the jargon of the computer world). Failure to know a minimum about computers can hurt you in job interviews. Personnel managers often cite their lack of enthusiasm for those teacher applicants who have not done their homework and who are naive about business and computers. Computer literacy and familiarity with computerese (the language that people in the computer field talk) will help you when interviewing.

You'll never know if you like Beef Wellington until you taste it; the same holds for the computer industry.

Opportunities Abound

Programming. Teachers of music, science, math, reading, home economics, and special needs, and teachers who are logical thinkers, organized, and methodical, become excellent programmers and find the writing of programs infinitely absorbing and stimulating. To determine your aptitude for programming, take one of the aptitude tests offered by an educational institution.

Programs are written in such languages as COBOL, BASIC, PASCAL, or FORTRAN. Most teachers have concentrated in COBOL, which is used in accounting. Since every business will have a computer in the coming years, for a job in programming it is probably best to specialize in this language. If you are scientifically oriented, talk to engineers already in the field to determine the best course of action for your interests. Almost all programmers know several languages and find it successively easier to learn new ones.

A program is basically a step-by-step set of instructions written in a language that the machine understands. Programs must follow a logical sequence and cannot skip any steps along the way. They differ in length, depending on the complexity of the problem to be solved. A lesson in long division, for instance, may take several weeks to write, and an entire arithmetic book, written as a software package, could take a year or more.

When a program has been written, it is run on the computer to see if it works smoothly. Sometimes there are bugs or glitches (errors) that need to be corrected. This phase is called debugging the program. (You may, for instance, have instructed the program to ask "How much is 2 × 2?" but left out the question mark. You would have to insert the question mark in the proper place.) When the program is debugged and runs smoothly, it is ready to be used.

As a programmer, you will sometimes work alone and sometimes perform as a member of a team. Those who develop good analytical skills and can understand the so-called gestalt of a problem may advance to the level of programmer/analyst or systems analyst. The analyst takes the major problem, separates it into smaller components, and works with programmers to find an effective solution. Systems analysts are in demand and earn an average of from $30,000 to $35,000 after a few years. Ex-teachers have advanced to these levels.

Software applications are so varied and seemingly endless—from the teaching of reading to the designing of robots—that the industry will provide programmers with career advancement and opportunities for years to come. Of all industries, the computer industry will permit more and more people to work at home, too, on terminals and other hardware connected to mainframes located elsewhere.

Although the best course of action is obtaining a computer science degree, colleges and computer institutes offer excellent certificate programs; make certain that the school you choose is accredited by your state board of education. The better the institution of learning, the better the opportunities for employment. Call a few local companies and ask the personnel manager to recommend a school that has the best program, and talk to a few graduates, if you can. Most of the better schools provide a placement service for graduates. Since the first job is often the most difficult to obtain, this can be a very valuable service. (By the way, the job of Placement Counselor and Admissions Counselor in these companies is often held by a former teacher.)

There are about 300,000 programmers presently working in the field (compared with 2.1 million teachers), so as a programmer you are a much rarer commodity. Once you become experienced, headhunters will be eager to place you at another company, at a considerable raise in pay. Starting salaries vary from $12,000 to $25,000, depending on the kind of education you received (from a computer institute to a highly-acclaimed college where you may have received a degree in computer science). Since there is a sixty percent turnover every eighteen months for programmers (programmers like money and challenge) and new openings are created at a faster rate than in other occupations, you should have a career that can provide upward mobility, management potential, and challenge.

Computer Consultant. The computer industry, because it is so young, has many holes and blanks waiting to be filled. It is these holes and blanks that have provided a stimulus for entrepreneurs, teachers included. Here is one success story to illustrate the point.

Success story: educational computer consultant. When computers were introduced into his school, John became involved right from the inception and soon found himself the resident expert. The principal, teachers, administrative staff, and students came to him with all their questions. Even parents sought his advice on the best kind of educational software and computer to buy. Within a few years, so many people requested his advice—free, of course—that he decided he had the basis for his own business.

Today John's business is only seven months old, but it is expanding every day. He consults on computers, software, and programming, and he trains new and old users in any phase of computer usage they request. His clientele ranges from principals to parents.

So much for the business-world myth that teachers are not aggressive!

I realize that it is difficult to make the decision to enter a new profession. Recalling the time when you decided to teach, you may remember the tenuous reasons that propelled you toward your particular degree. In the beginning your teaching may not have been so much a question of *suitability,* as it was *adaptability;* and so it is with programming. Many former teachers, after taking a first course, however, become hooked on programming, especially those teachers who make up their minds to be adaptable. Even if you never work as a programmer, it may be advisable to take courses because it has been proven that teachers who have done so have made the easiest transitions into technical writing, training, educational publishing, and other related fields—including their own businesses.

The best states in which to find jobs with computer manufacturers are California, Illinois, Massachusetts, Michigan, New York, Ohio, Pennsylvania, and Texas, but every state has opportunities.

Technical Writing. If you have ever researched and written a term paper, an article, or a story, or have been an English, math, science, or music teacher, you can learn to be a technical writer.

Companies who sell computers, software packages, and peripherals publish manuals that explain the way their equipment is operated. These manuals are written by technical writers, many of them former teachers.

Since the computer world is always in a state of flux, because of the constant change in technology, these manuals need to be updated frequently in order to provide the user with the latest set of instructions.

Working in conjunction with engineers, programmers, drafters, graphic artists, photographers, production staff, and editors, technical writers gain insight into the information to be presented and the format of the publication. At first, the technical language and the information is strange, but just like any other skill—skiing, for example—mastery becomes easier each day. A good writer develops an interesting style and is able to explain clearly a set of instructions that can be easily followed.

If you decide to become a tech writer, enroll in the best program you can locate at your local college or computer institute.

After taking preparatory courses, teachers have started writing and editing manuals on a part-time basis, while teaching. This is an excellent idea for you to try because it will look good on your resume. In addition, since part-time employment is a goal for some people, technical writing can fulfill the objective.

If you gain free-lance experience and have writing samples to submit, attending a high tech job fair could be productive; companies hire experienced people at these fairs. Without computer or tech writing credentials the possibility of receiving a job offer is low, but a few former teachers have had success. What did they do? They refused to take "No" for an answer. They used their tried-and-true powers of persuasion to break down arguments. They persisted. And they were hired for technical writing training programs; rare, but true. At a starting salary of about $20,000, could you learn to be persuasive, too?

Technical writers are in demand and will continue to be in short supply for the foreseeable future. In this field it is not unusual to become a supervisor or a manager very quickly and to earn $30,000 and more within a few years.

Former teachers have opened their own firms writing and printing manuals for other companies.

You don't believe, do you, that "You can't teach an old dog new tricks?"

Sales. Since all companies have a vested interest in selling their products, and there is always a shortage of salespeople, one of the best and easiest ways to crack the computer field is through sales.

If there is any correlation between one field and another, it surely exists between teaching and sales. The same high level of personality traits that made you successful in teaching will make you successful in sales: verbal ability, clarity of explanation, a one-on-one helping relationship, rapport with people, and satisfaction in doing a job well done.

The sales field offers some values that teachers treasure: a high degree of autonomy over your modus operandi and your time, and the freedom to travel if you so desire.

Sales people can work in small computer retail stores or for manufacturers, research companies involved with computers, advertising and public relations companies, or computer accounting service firms; you can investigate those companies most closely aligned with your interests. Teachers also sell computers to schools. Income from sales positions can be the highest among any positions. It is not unusual for people to start at $20,000 and to double their salaries within the year by accruing commissions. A young woman who began selling computers five years ago now earns over $100,000. Hers is only one of many success stories.

Since IBM has recently entered the personal computer market and has only a 3.9 percent market share, you might find sales openings with this company as it makes an attempt to capture a bigger market share.

Those teachers who want an express ticket into the computer world and who are eager for financial success should jump aboard the sales train and enjoy a fascinating trip meeting fascinating people.

Training. You have read the preceding chapter on training so are now aware of this exciting, creative career. The computer industry, which is growing at a faster rate than most industries, will be a seedbed for an untold number of new training jobs. It is not too soon for you to start taking a computer literacy course and others courses that will be a door-opener for you in this growing industry.

You may be thinking: What do I know about computers? How can I ever learn to teach in this field?

Just remember that when the computer industry was inaugurated, no one knew much about computers. Every trainer (who was probably a former teacher) started in his or her position with practically no computer knowledge. Day by day, little by little, information was studied and learned. The computer field changes so rapidly that yesterday's information can be useless today. That is where the trainer's usefulness resides: in explaining and teaching—exactly what you do best. After you've learned the basics, you may want to start your computer career working in a local retail computer store. There are two advantages that may accrue from such employment.

1. Your next employer will be more likely to hire you if your resume indicates previous employment in the computer field, and

2. You may be lucky enough to have a president of a company enter the store for a demonstration. In conversation, you may discover he needs someone to train his data-entry clerks in computer usage. Voilà! Your training career begins. You won't be the first person to get your big opportunity in this manner.

If you can't find a job as a trainer, look into these other possibilities in the training departments: Documentation Specialist,

Curriculum Developer, Sales Trainer, Demonstration Specialist, Coordinator of Media Activities, Script Writer, Coordinator of Materials, Training Assistant, Student Advisor, Photographer, Artist, and other titles you may discover while reading the ads. Visit a large company; meet the trainers and talk to them about the variety of positions in this creative field.

Salaries in training departments start at $20,000 or $25,000 and accelerate rapidly.

If you loved teaching, you'll adore training.

Computer Education Publishing. The more you keep your eyes and ears open to the computer world, the more astonished you will be at the career varieties that will surface. Here's a veritable gem.

Since the computer industry is still new, entrepreneurs are having a field day. It seems as though every week a new company springs up (usually formed by breakaways from similar but larger companies). The need for software to fill all of society's demands is so great that everyone is jumping on the bandwagon to fill it.

One of the needs that has caught the fancy of educators is courseware, the name given to educational computer software written for children and adults. If you have been seeking a career with relevance to the educational world, you can't get much closer than writing courseware for students.

Because teachers know how people learn best and are familiar with school subjects, publishers of courseware need teachers; teachers know how to build in the proper rewards for correct answers, too. It is interesting to see how the personality of the teacher-programmer shines through the courseware as his or her style is developed.

Into the finished product or packaging of courseware goes artwork, scripts, editing, and curriculum knowledge—all transferrable skills that teachers possess or are learning. These companies also hire salespeople, coordinators, and other administrators. The value of these companies is that they are often eager to have part-time employees, so you may be able to get a foot in the door either before you quit teaching or if you are seeking to work part-time. If you become really good at writing programs, you may consider putting them on diskettes, forming your own company, and marketing your products; teachers have already started this kind of business. (Husbands and wives, when both are interested, become a strong entrepreneurial team.)

Production or Publications. For art teachers or those disposed to art or photography: the computer world holds a place for you.

Computer companies have their own publication departments in which the first or completed drafts of their manuals are prepared. In this department there are photographers, artists, writers, coordinators, and managers. If you are creative, you may be able to find a career in such a department. Management positions are readily available to the experienced.

Word Processing. Some people have the notion that to use a word processor you have to be a programmer. These same people think that you have to be a programmer to use any computer. Neither of the above statements is true. To use a word processor, which is a simple form of a computer, you have to know how to type and then learn some easy, basic ways of manipulating the information on the video screen. Almost all reporters and writers use word processors today.

Despite statements to the contrary, getting a job as a word processor per se is tantamount to getting a job as a typist. (Note that both the computer and the person who uses the computer is called a word processor. Sometimes the person who uses the computer is referred to as the word-processing operator.) The advantages of taking a job as a word processor, however, are numerous. First of all, since there is a celebrated shortage, you could find a job immediately at an hourly rate of up to $8.00. By having immediate access to a company, you will be able to discover opportunities sooner than you would have done otherwise, because some jobs never hit the newspapers. You will also begin to form a network of people who may be helpful to you in the future. If you work for a temporary employment agency and change jobs every few weeks or months, your network will grow, your horizons will widen, and your opportunities to hear about and apply for something else will multiply exponentially. If you are lucky, you will be asked to stay on as a trainer of other word-processing secretaries in the company; this has happened to many teachers.

Word processing as a career can have its advantages. Because there is such a demand, you can work during the winter and take time off during the summer, as you did before. Or you can work part-time as a word processor in order to make the money to pay for essentials or for a hobby. Not many jobs have this option, but this one does.

To continue to applaud the ingenuity of teachers, I must tell you that they have opened their own word-processing training centers. Companies cannot train word-processing secretaries fast enough, so private companies have been formed to fill the gap. These companies train employees and also hire employees to do some of their client companies' word-processing overloads. One company I know also trains ex-teachers and others who want to be word processors. When the first group of trainees graduated from this company, they needed jobs. What did the owner do? She added on a temporary employment agency and placed the newly-trained word processors with companies who were hungry for their skills! Needless to say, this is not only a lucrative business but a source of employment for many other teachers.

Teachers of business subjects in particular should be reading carefully because this field is allied to their own. Teachers who have worked for such companies have often ended as trainers in the companies they were serving, or have found careers as counselors, recruiters, or salespeople with larger companies.

Computer Operator. Since the first computer was put to commercial use in 1951, computer systems have infiltrated every part of our daily lives. Among the variety of computer-related jobs is that of the computer operator, who works directly with the machine and facilitates the processing and completion of a particular program.

The operation of all data systems involves entering data and instructions (or input), operating the computer, and retrieving the results (or output). Input needs to be prepared by either a keypunch operator or a data typist, who translates the data into a machine-readable format, usually by means of a keyboard similar to a typewriter's.

Computer operators must have a certain amount of specialized knowledge, such as knowledge of a code language, but some organizations are willing to train employees on the job. There are plenty of courses at vocational schools and colleges, as well as seminars held by business firms offering computer training opportunities. Computer operators can earn up to $25,000 and can advance to Lead Operator, a management position.

The Computer Doctor and the Serviceperson. Economists are predicting that the computer technician will be one of the most sought-after employees as we approach the 1990s, the time when computers will be ubiquitous. The technician will be like your old-fashioned country practitioner, a so-called Computer Doctor, who will make house calls to cure computer ills.

Computerland, one of the largest computer franchises, reports that the average technician earns $22,360 a year and that top Computer Doctors earn almost $35,000.

For teachers who already have their bachelor's degrees, a one- or two-year program at a technical school would provide them with most of the technical basics. There is statistical proof that this service industry is growing very rapidly.

If you are a person who has always been the fixer in your house, you may want to consider another technical field that has a shortage of service people: the office copying machine field. Most companies conduct intensive training on their equipment before they send employees to local businesses to inspect and repair their machines. The new breed of technician wears a business suit and looks like an ivy leaguer. These field positions offer mobility as the technician travels from company to company. This kind of a job provides excellent exposure because one meets people in many settings—universities, hospitals, banks, and business—and it may be a door opener.

Technician positions can lead rapidly to management, where salaries of $40,000 and $50,000 are commonplace.

Other Possibilities. In computer companies there is a constant need for employees in all the other jobs you will find explained in other chapters. When you are computer literate, you will be valuable to companies in any of the following fields: recruiting, personnel, accounting, advertising, marketing, and so on.

Who asked whether there is life after teaching?

4. Careers in Personnel

If you want to get into a growing field in which you may also grow professionally, consider the personnel field. Company expansion, increased employer commitment, and affirmative action programs (see Chapter 9) have created a favorable outlook for employment in this field. I could devote an entire chapter to describing teachers who have talked their way into personnel positions by convincing a manager or a president of a small company that their skills were essential to the organization. Here is one success story.

Success story: the personnel generalist. Donna came into Plantech, Inc., as a temporary worker. The firm was relatively new, and there was no personnel department; the president, the accountant, and a secretary shared personnel responsibilities.

What did Donna know about the functions of a personnel department? Nothing. But she saw an opportunity and seized it, convincing the president (and herself!) that her teaching experience and her desire to produce results would be a winning combination.

As a personnel generalist Donna had to learn a great deal. The generalist has to perform all the functions of the department, usually with the assistance of a secretary. Many people in personnel agree that the generalist who juggles a potpourri of assignments has an interesting job because, like a one-person band, "You get to do everything yourself."

Donna gleaned some information about her job from the people who had had the responsibility before she arrived, but much of it was acquired through contact with other personnel generalists and through seminars and workshops that the company paid for and permitted her to attend.

What are the responsibilities of the generalist?

- Overall planning for the welfare of all employees.
- Interviewing and screening of prospective employees.
- Orientation of new employees (introductions, explanations of company policies, and so on).
- Consulting with managers to determine their employment needs.
- Processing of benefits, claims, and insurance forms.
- Setting standards for and monitoring performance of employees.
- Counseling employees.
- Writing and placing employment advertising.
- Keeping employees abreast of new information.

Today, after three years, Donna is earning more than $25,000 a year at the same company. Were there risks? Were there fears to overcome? Many—but there were many rewards, too.

Benefits or Compensation Assistant. As companies grow, their personnel departments must also expand in order to accommodate the increased workload. When this occurs, one of the newly-created openings is often in the field of compensation and benefits. Without experience you could not qualify for a job as a compensation or benefits specialist, but most teachers could qualify for an assistant's position and learn on the job. The person in this job deals with wage and salary surveys and administration, writes job descriptions, and learns and explains the health benefits, retirement plans, tuition reimbursement, and other employee-related benefits. Try to get a job in this field, learn as much as you can, prove youself, and look around for the opportunity to move into a higher-income spot. Many companies are committed to helping thiir employees accomplish this career goal of upward mobility. (If yours isn't, move on.) Benefits and Compensation Specialists are in great demand. After only three years one specialist is earning $35,000—a former teacher, of course!

Recruiter. If you are a good judge of people and have strong communications skills, you may wish to hunt out the well-paying job of recruiter, another position in the personnel department. A recruiter hires technical or skilled people—engineers, technicians, chemists, and so forth—and may travel to colleges and other states to conduct interviews. When you examine the Sunday newspaper ads pertaining to this title, the requirements may seem beyond you. Don't believe it! The only two prerequisites are to relate well to people and to convince the interviewer that you can do the job.

One former teacher with whom I deal is a very successful industrial recruiter. How did she get her first start in industry? Easily. When she heard that a certain company was hiring, she walked right in the door and asked to speak with the employment manager. Convinced, herself, that her interviewing skills and instincts were good, she was able to convince the manager that she learned quickly and would learn the jargon that was necessary to recruit technical employees. After a second interview, the job was hers at $22,000 a year. I strongly recommend this approach. (See Chapter 7 for additional information on recruiting.)

Employment Interviewer. If you have all the skills listed above, even to a lesser degree, try seeking the job of employment interviewer. This position involves working with other departments to establish their employment needs, writing and placing employment ads, and interviewing and hiring prospective candidates. Jobs like this can be found in banks, hospitals, industry, and government. Don't wait to see ads appear in the newspaper; make your own opportunity: the competition, if you use this method, is minimal. Look for companies that advertise heavily. Go in and tell them that you'd like to help them interview candidates. After observing for one day, you'll be able to do it your-self. *Be resourceful. Be bold. Be confident.*

Human Resources Director. One of the up-and-coming jobs in industry is that of the human resources director, a high-level managerial position that is often of vice-presidential rank. In many companies the title is director or vice president of personnel.

Although the responsibilities vary from company to company, the human resources director is essentially responsible for the overall planning and policymaking in such areas as manpower projection, utilization and development of employee potential, institution of management training programs, and interpretation and administration of government regulations. To implement these programs, the director hires generalists and specialists.

The human resources director is responsive to the needs of all employees, regardless of position in the company. After all, employers want to guard their most vital resource: people.

A teacher could assist a human resources director in training, communicating company policy to employees, administering tests, compiling statistics, and organizing data. College teachers and administrators who have worked in placement or career counseling as corporate liaison administrators or as principals of schools are in a good position to create this job in a rapidly grow-ing company, or in an established company without this type of a department. See the reference section of your library for lists of manufacturers in your geographical area, and learn whether there is a gap in their corporate structures; you could fill it. If you plan to move into this field, you must do the necessary re-search, and perhaps take a few courses in organizational man-agement and human resources. Most colleges have an evening division and give excellent courses in many aspects of personnel. In addition to the decided advantage you will have over bach-elor's recipients without personnel and business courses is the advantage of mingling with practicing professionals. You could meet someone who will offer you a job or could introduce you to someone else who is a good contact. Business courses are a definite asset when applying for a job in industry; when you are interviewed, be sure to mention them. Include them on your re-sume, too.

Even in a recession, hospitals, banks, and some companies continue to grow and must add to their personnel departments. Watch the financial pages of your newspaper for earnings reports, and use business reference books to find organizations with good earnings trends.

Why is personnel a propitious field for you? Every ability you possess as a teacher can be put into action in the personnel department. And if your job entails reporting to top management, you may be able to use your teacher's powers of persuasion to increase the company's commitment to its employees.

For the very well-qualified individual who can become proficient in union negotiations, wage and salary administration, manpower planning, finance, and macroeconomics, the salary level is boundless.

In a field in which many people have been promoted into higher positions because of longevity or simply because they were there, a person with ambition, sensitivity, skill, and savoir faire can easily rise to the top.

Salaries in this field vary with experience, but $15,000 to $20,000 is average for entry-level employees, and they can start higher, if the applicant has a master's degree.

5. Creative Careers

Many people choose the teaching profession because of its tremendous creative potential. These same people can find career satisfaction outside the world of teaching, in dozens of jobs that combine creative talents with the skills that teachers frequently possess. All jobs require creativity, but some use more originality than others.

Public Relations Specialist. If you took all your talents and fed them into a computer, one of the career fields that the computer would spew out would be public relations, a field that reflects a perfect composite of a teacher's talents:

- Creative flair
- Ability to use language effectively
- Self-confidence
- A gregarious personality
- Initiative

Doesn't this description fit you?

Public relations departments are found in hospitals, uni-

31

versities, businesses, and government, as well as in a variety of organizations in the community. Many small public relations firms have sprung up recently. A few operate out of people's homes. Most companies have a speciality: a company may specialize in marketing authors; a larger firm may create a total image for a new computer company, such as Apple, designing the logo and writing stories about the company that are sent to the media. The purpose is to keep a person or a company in the eye of the public.

At the highest level of responsibility there will probably be a vice president, if the company is large. Down in the ranks will be writers, a research staff, interviewers, photographers, and video experts; take your pick, according to your talents.

Working for a smaller institution could have its advantages. There may not be a V.P., but the V.I.P. could be you. If there is a pro who moves on to greener territory, then guess who's IT?

Here's a true story to illustrate this case in point:

Success story: public relations. Selma was at a loss when her teaching job was suddenly terminated. She talked to all her friends who were working and asked them to think hard: Were there any business changes they knew of that would create a job opening? Yes. A new hospital had just opened. Selma discovered a part-time job in the newly-created public relations department of the hospital. She applied for the position, bringing with her a portfolio of writing samples, which she had saved from her class-room teaching days and from outside activities. She was hired because her skills and personality suited the role.

Selma's responsibilities included interviewing doctors and other staff members, writing human interest stories, and supervising the production of a newsletter—all new experiences using old skills. Her main responsibility, however, was to contact the media in order to publicize the hospital's commitment to community-wide service.

After a year Selma changed employers, obtained a full-time position, and increased her salary immensely. She became a public relations specialist for a prestigious department store chain dealing with the public and the community, a job she loved. When her boss left she became the director.

Selma used very good sense in her search for employment. She told all her friends that she had lost her job and asked them for leads. The likelihood of finding something was thus much greater than if she had just answered ads. The portfolio of printed materials started during her teaching days was used as a sales tool; save your materials, too!

After a year, when Selma decided to change jobs, to avoid risking financial loss she looked for the new one while she continued to work at the old one. Keep this in mind.

Is there a stigma attached to changing jobs after a year? Not any more, if a good reason can be offered. Years ago people stayed in jobs forever. Today the average length of time in one job is from eighteen months to two years, especially in the computer field.

When I asked Selma why she had decided originally to become a teacher, she responded:

"What else was there? I couldn't think of anything else then. Neither could my friends. Now I know of many jobs I could hold."

You can see now that limited thinking is a mistake. There is another job out there for you, once you start to think positively. Formulate a plan—and act on it!

Publishing. Textbook publishers seek the expertise that only a teacher can offer: actual working experience within a classroom environment. Whom else should they hire to test the quality of their elementary texts? Only a teacher who is familiar with the responses and ideas of children can judge the practicality of a reader or a math text. Teachers are employed to do curriculum development, to edit manuscripts, and to market and sell these books to former colleagues. For many teachers, selling books is the perfect occupation because of the flexibility of working hours—part-time or full-time—the independence it permits, and the teacher's familiarity with educators and educational institutions. Educators feel confident and comfortable buying books from ex-teachers.

Many publishing firms are now under government scrutiny to promote their editors (especially women) to administrative positions, a practice to which they were not previously committed. The need to comply with equal opportunity laws will create opportunities for new people to enter the profession.

Success story: publishing. Ellen was an English teacher who moonlighted as an editor for a physician who was writing a medical textbook. Ellen's job as editor was basically to correct the grammar, improve the style, and put the manuscript into an interesting format that was readable and understandable. Ellen's father had been a physician—a factor that gave her a familiarity with medical terminology, but it was her interest in medicine that propelled her to edit medical books.

When Ellen decided to seek a full-time position as an editor, she was encouraged to interview with a major publisher. She brought along with her the book that she was editing. The vice president was very much impressed and hired her as an associate medical editor at $20,000. Her responsibilities were to deal with authors and encourage them to write textbooks, edit, coordinate publications, and attend book fairs. Later she changed jobs and became a vice president, a post that would be a feather in anybody's cap.

The competition for jobs in publishing is keen; yet teachers have made successful transitions into this field. Salaries are low to start, from $12,000 to $15,000. One former teacher who moved into marketing earns $35,000 today.

Educational Materials. The need to stimulate and creatively educate the student of today has fostered a proliferation of companies dedicated to the development of innovative educational products. Exciting, original work is being produced in learning games, learning modules, graphics, films, math and science kits—all magnets to attract and educate elementary and secondary school pupils and adults, too.

The proliferation of the computer in the classroom has created a new kind of material called schoolware or courseware, terms that are take-offs from the word *software*. Schoolware and courseware are learning programs written for the education market. Since educational materials are so closely allied with your profession, if you are a creative teacher you will find fertile soil in which to grow in an educationally-oriented company. Are you a writer, an artist, a creator of filmstrips, a photographer? Can you design curricula or develop games? If you can do any of these things, a publisher of educational materials may be your answer.

Where can these companies be found? The most recent directories, including one on computers, are listed in the reference section at the back of this book: *The El-Hi Market 1984–89* and *Micro-Computer Hardware and Software in the El-Hi Market 1983–87.* Your library may have a copies of these studies, which list all companies in the United States producing educational materials. If there is a publishing company nearby, it may be producing similar materials or may have a copy of one of these books; call that company. If nothing turns up, all is not lost; look in the Yellow Pages of your telephone directory under:

- Educational films
- Educational equipment
- Graphics for educators
- Educational research
- Research and development

Even if you are not particularly creative, remember that these companies hire administrators and salespeople, too. Whatever your leaning, there is enough variety to strike a fruitful balance. Best of all, though, you will feel at home there because many ex-teachers work for these publishers. (See Chapter 3 for more information.)

The In-House Newsletter Writer. The in-house newsletter is a public relations instrument found wherever there is information to be disseminated. Employees in industry, government, education, business, social service, and just about anywhere receive newsletters used as vehicles to convey news they need to know. Look around the house or in your IN box; you'll find one, too, no doubt. Newsletters are produced by the gas company, every bank, most industrial companies, the real estate association, the teachers association—they are ubiquitous. Someone has to write and produce these newsletters, and it could be you.

One of the best ways to find out about this kind of work is to join the National Association of Communicators. By joining a local branch, you will receive a directory of all the newsletter editors in your geographical area. Call on your branch of this association and see where the call leads. Of course, the association sends out a newsletter, too—one that is valuable to you because it contains job openings. One teacher visited the office of the president of this association. He didn't receive a job offer there but he was given five leads, two of which did turn into job offers! His career as a communicator had begun. Helped by a successful person, he, in turn, has helped others when he became a success—an altruistic game that many professionals enjoy playing.

Radio and Television Specialists. Programming departments of television and radio stations produce daily and weekly shows and cover special events. In these departments are news directors who plan and supervise the coverage of newsworthy events. There are also news writers who write the copy for the newscaster to read. In addition, reporters gather newsworthy information and interview people. There are also continuity directors who are responsible for writing and editing scripts, directors, associate directors, producers, associate producers, and program assistants who assemble and coordinate the shows. Community and public affairs directors supervise, write, or act as hosts of public affairs programs.

Entry into some of these positions requires minimal experience. One of my most exciting success stories concerns a former teacher who worked as an intern at a television studio. She was so well liked and made herself so well known that she was hired as an associate producer on a very popular program. Seek out internship and re-entry programs in your area for this field or any other field. Internship programs usually end up with at least half the interns placed and provide a good base for networking.

A liberal arts degree is desirable, although some employers want broadcasting or journalism background. There are new stations cropping up all the time, adding to the United States' existing 1,149 television stations and 9,320 radio stations. There is a lot of competition out there, but adults often have the edge over young graduates because of their maturity.

Audio-Visual Specialist. Teachers have been trained to use the audio-visual equipment that almost every school possesses. Opportunities for employment in the audio-visual field exist in colleges and hospitals, as well as in companies that sell equipment to schools. (See Educational Materials on pages 34–35.) Few teachers know that most businesses and industrial firms have audio-visual departments, too, where films are made to train salespeople, managers, technicians, clerical workers, and customers. If you can learn to operate and repair the equipment, you will have an additional sales tool with which to buy yourself a job.

Exciting, creative work is being done in this field, much of it by teachers who have discovered the growing opportunities in it. Companies are producing scripts and films to use with both customers and employees. Salary levels are commensurate with those of experienced teachers.

Advertising. Products are brought to the attention of the public by advertising agencies, which create for their clients campaigns to be used in magazines, newspapers, television, and radio. Advertising agencies can be found in small towns and urban centers, with the major agencies located in the cities. Agencies prepare advertising for companies of every size, from retail stores to manufacturers of major consumer items. Since the advertising industry is expected to grow faster than other fields, this may be the time to prepare yourself by taking several graduate courses at your local college, especially if the following description fits your talents.

Copywriter. If you have a flair for writing compelling paragraphs that convey the advantage of a product or service, try advertising copywriting.

Should you select a small advertising agency or newspaper? Perhaps, because there your work could have more variety. Once you have proven that you have a lively curiosity about the products, can get to the heart of the products' benefits, and can consistently turn out original, eye-catching copy, you can expect rather high recognition and rewards.

Don't expect a fancy starting salary, because this is a highly competitive field. If you demonstrate an unusual talent and propensity to work hard, however, promotions can be rapid.

If you work for a large advertising agency, your early assignments—to test your skills—will consist of writing a paragraph or two. To prepare for the assignment you will want to learn as much as you can about the product. If you can express the advantages of the product in a fresh, memorable way, in words that complement the graphics, you're on your way!

Account Executive. One of the goals of employees in advertising is the position of account executive, which deals directly with the client. This highly desirable and competitive management position is not held by a neophyte; it is held by an experienced employee who has proven his or her creative, interpersonal, and business skills.

The account executive is the liaison between the agency and the client. Together, they plan an advertising campaign that will involve artists and copywriters and other groups. The account executive monitors the progress from the inception through the delivery, working under the pressure of deadlines.

In-House Advertising. Many large companies have their own advertising departments, which are usually under the umbrella of the marketing department. They, too, have an entire complement of artists, writers, market researchers, publications specialists, and account executives. When there is a need for television coverage of a highly sophisticated project, these companies will work in conjunction with advertising firms, too. Needless to say, the contact creates a network for a future exchange of personnel! (As you can see, there is more mobility in the business world than in teaching.)

Starting salaries in advertising average about $15,000 to $20,000, but M.B.A.s can receive up to $25,000. After three or four years, you could easily earn $30,000 and more, if you are good at the job. Breaking into this field is easiest in smaller companies; teachers have had success.

Technical Writing. Many former teachers have made this position into their newly-adopted profession. Technical writing is demanding, constantly changing, and often right in the middle of state-of-the-art technology.

Technical writers can be involved in more than computer manuals. What are some of the fields in which they get involved?

Technical writers are employed in electronics, the federal government, advertising agencies, the consumer industry (like cosmetics and games), the food industry, the chemical industry, the petroleum industry, and most other industries.

Technical writers put scientific information into language that can be understood. They may also research and edit technical materials and produce publications and instructional media productions. (For instance, the Air Force may need to produce a film to recruit military personnel.)

Writers prepare scripts for training films. They may also write speeches, news releases, and public relations releases, or develop advertising copy for exhibits or displays. Once you are employed in a department, you could easily work on one type of assignment or another, often wearing different hats, if you show the talent.

The backgrounds required of technical writers are very diverse: music, science, liberal arts, biology, chemistry, and mathematics. If your interest is in writing, you can learn the technical jargon; this fact has been proven.

Creative employment-seeking pays off, too. If you have pursued a hobby thoroughly, like stamp collecting, and have the ability to write, you could search for a company in your town that issues a catalog for collectors. I looked in my Yellow Pages for you and found a giant company nearby that I hadn't known existed. If I were a collector and seeking a job, I'd walk in with my scrapbooks and start talking.

If you have a background in English, it is also possible to seek and find employment as an editor—and often a teacher of others—in the technical writing department. Everywhere the embarrassing discovery is being made that scientists and technical people often cannot write clearly or logically. The technical editor must be able to learn enough of the jargon produced by technical employees (engineers, for example) to translate it into understandable terms.

Serious staff shortages abound today in these departments, and these shortages are expected to continue. Salaries start at $20,000 and increase rapidly. (See Chapter 3, too.)

Photography. Photography is a field that has more than meets the eye. Photographers work in industry photographing equipment, products, and employees at work. The photos are then used in annual reports, newsletters, and press releases. I have placed an ex-teacher in the printed circuit industry, where he works in a laboratory using photographic and etching processes. Photographers work for department stores, hospitals, colleges, government, and the media, photographing models, clothing, news, and sports events. Almost a third of all photographers are self-employed, largely because of the low start-up costs and because of their need for autonomy.

The most highly-paid people in this field have developed a speciality for which there was a demand that few people could fill. A new company is editing customers' home movies and is making a success of it.

Most employment in this field started from a deep interest in photography as a hobby. Combined with creative thinking, good marketing techniques, and talent, it can be a fascinating, lucrative profession.

Interior Designer/Decorator. The interior designer can be either a man or woman who creates aesthetically pleasing living areas. He or she may work on private homes or commercial buildings, and may plan and supervise the design and furniture arrangements. To enter this field you must be able to provide scaled drawings in order to obtain a license to practice interior design; decorators are not licensed and need not have this skill, although they may possess it.

Designers are expected to make drawings that contain furniture, accessories, and structural changes. They look for and buy the furnishings, supervise the work of installing them, and often design furniture. Both designers and decorators deal with paperwork—placing orders, figuring estimates, billing customers, and maintaining records. Interior designers and decorators can work alone or with other employees or partners, in large or small design companies, or for department and furniture stores. They can also work for architects, antique dealers, or furniture manufacturers, and can even write feature articles for magazines.

Formal training is unnecessary for a decorator—good taste is the only requirement. An interior designer will be better able to withstand competition, however, or be more able to enter a sophisticated company after taking special courses in design, art, or architecture, or after studying in a three year design program.

In running a decorating business you can employ yourself, set your own hours, and teach, too, in a local school or college— as does my friend Frieda, an ex–home economics teacher, who has recently been promoted to Program Director at the college where she teaches.

In writing about creative careers, I cannot help thinking about the expression "cream will rise to the top"—a rather dated expression for those accustomed only to homogenized milk. The expression persists in my mind, however, when I think about the talents of teachers. I thoroughly believe that a teacher who desires to find a rewarding new career and who works at achieving the goal will be successful, no matter what the background. I know, too, that former teachers will bring creativity to their new work, whatever and wherever it may be.

6. Educational And Nonprofit Organizations

Are you aware that colleges and the nonprofit community are large-scale employers of part-time and full-time administrators? This is a good field to investigate for those teachers who may wish to remain in education while making better use of their managerial talents and for those turned off by business. The good news is that although there is a declining young student population, more adults are attending colleges than ever before, especially community colleges and continuing education divisions of colleges.

College Administration

One well-known university publishes a weekly job listing with an average of fifteen openings for professional and support staff, many of which go unfilled week after week. So don't overlook the nations's 3,000 community, junior, private, city, and state colleges and universities. Although there is competition for positions, the best opportunities are in the growing system of community colleges, rapidly expanding continuing education divisions, and private schools. Economic necessity has brought a need for specific, immediate training. Small, private, and other technical schools can educate students in a shorter period of time and for less money than can other institutions, so opportunities are opening up there in administration.

What are the educational requirements for these jobs? Contrary to what might be expected, many college administrative positions require no more than a liberal arts degree, although a master's degree is desirable. The most prestigious positions, such as president, academic dean, and dean of graduate studies, generally require a Ph.D.

Below are the administrative positions recently listed as open by personnel departments of colleges throughout the United States. Don't forget that assistant or associate directors are hired for many of these positions as well. The openings for administrative positions are advertised in the weekly periodical *Chronicle of Higher Education,* but you can benefit personally by getting to know your local college administrators.

- Alumni Director
- Director of Financial Aid
- Director of Transitional Year Program (to aid minority students)
- Education Programming Assistant
- Dean of Admissions
- Director of Placement
- Dean of Students
- Director of Student Affairs
- Head Resident Counselor (live-in position)
- Personnel Manager
- Director of Development (fundraising)
- Affirmative Action Officer

Why is it that these positions and others are open to B.A. candidates and do not necessarily require a higher degree?

All colleges operate under budgetary constraints. When a director of admissions leaves the college after a period of five or ten years, the salary, because of annual increments, is high. When advertising the new opening, the personnel department will drop the salary back, in keeping with its policy of paying less to a new administrator in order to balance the budget. Salaries can start at $12,000 (B.A.) or $15,000 (M.A.).

Teachers who are aware of this information can use it to their advantage. Certainly, a visit to a personnel department of a nearby college can help to clarify the requirements and determine your eligibility for employment. Colleges are more receptive than any institution to your teaching credentials.

Student Personnel Positions

There is a myriad of people employed in colleges working under the heading *student services*. This staff is concerned with housing, social, cultural, recreational, and other student needs. Some of these positions are outlined below, but you will find others if you visit schools and make inquiries.

Not all colleges have been committed to internship programs, but the need for field experience before entering the job market is becoming apparent. You could create a position as an internship developer (a position that I have held) if your local college has no such position.

Admissions Officer. Admissions officers, recruiters, or counselors promote and assess students' choices for college education. They work closely with people of all backgrounds and ages outside the college, as well as with a variety of college personnel, as part of student services.

Admissions counselors interview and evaluate prospective students and process their applications. Recruiters travel to high schools and junior colleges to make their college programs known. Older students and community residents are often sought by a college as well. Within the college the counselors work closely with faculty, administrators, financial aid personnel, and public relations staff to determine policies.

Generally speaking, a bachelor's degree in a social science field and sometimes a master's in student personnel work are required for these positions. It is always an advantage for the admissions worker to have graduated from the college that employs him or her.

Employment prospects for college student personnel officers

are likely to be competitive through this decade. Admissions counselors will, however, be among those least affected by college budget constraints, because colleges are recruiting actively for students.

Career Planning and Placement Counselors. Placement personnel assist students in all phases of career decisions. They help students examine their interests and goals and consider alternative careers and further training. Counselors must keep abreast of job market development and maintain contact with industry and government personnel departments and recruiters. Many people have gotten their start in industry via this route. After having met people in industry, they were able to find an opening there.

Guidance Counselors. Counselors help students with personal, educational, and vocational problems. A counselor may deal with a variety of student situations—loneliness, desire to leave college, failure in academic work, marriage problems, or problems with drug dependencies. Counselors administer psychological tests, conduct classes, and assist with the training of residence hall staff (another opportunity for employment if you can live on the campus).

Dean of Students. The dean of students heads the student personnel program. Duties include evaluating the changing needs of the students and helping the college president develop institutional policies to meet those needs. The dean usually supervises a group of associate or assistant deans who are in charge of specific programs. (In small schools, a B.A. may be acceptable.)

Financial Aid Personnel. Financial aid personnel advise students on where and how to obtain financial support for their education. Financial aid personnel must manage the paperwork and keep well-informed about the sources of aid, including scholarships, grants, employment, fellowships, and teaching and research assistantships. Close interaction with administrators and with the admissions, business, and academic office staff is often required.

Other aspects of student personnel work include the tasks performed by student activities workers, student housing officers, and foreign student advisors. Titles vary from one institution to another, as does the level of responsibility for each position, but you will find student personnel workers on every academic campus across the country.

Student personnel work involves working closely with people of all backgrounds and ages and requires a certain amount of emotional stability and the ability to function under pressure. Training requirements vary, but a teaching degree is a highly desirable qualification. Specialized courses in counseling and psychology, a familiarity with data processing, and experience as an intern are valuable assets. Added competition for jobs may increase the desirability of an M.A.

Employment prospects for all such positions are likely to be competitive through the decade as budgets tighten on all college campuses. Along with admissions officers, financial aid workers are least likely to be affected. As community colleges continue to reach out to adults, in order to train them for new positions and also to fulfill the colleges' mission of making lifelong learning possible, more job opportunities may be forthcoming.

Corporate Liaison Specialist

Colleges are dependent upon corporate clients for research and development funds in both scientific and humanistic fields. The Corporate Liaison Specialist meets with such people as corporate officers, chemists, and engineers to discuss their research needs, which might be for a non-toxic hair color, a faster computer, or a study of the differentiation between babies' cries. The information that is obtained from these meetings is then provided to the college's research departments. In this manner, new or additional funding is secured for the college's professors who are involved in state-of-the-art technology.

Hired for this position are people who have the skills and confidence to work with others on the corporate level. Often, alumni make the best candidates because they are familiar with the college's philosophy and programs. Some travel may be required; salaries vary from $12,000 to $20,000.

Grants Administrator

What kind of work does a grants administrator do? A grant (of money) may be provided by the federal government to a university to do a three-year feasibility study on a health center for community elderly, for instance. The professor who received the grant would ask the university's personnel department to place an ad in the newspaper for a Grant Administrator (sometimes called Program Administrator or Coordinator). This job is well within the range of a teacher's abilities because it involves organizing and documenting the activities that will take place during the length of the grant and coordinating the program. Don't be afraid to inquire about and apply for these professional positions, which will challenge your skills, provide you with a wealth of new contacts, be extremely interesting—and pay well, too (in the $20,000-plus range).

Although these positions last only from one to three years, they can become career positions because all colleges, hospitals, and agencies receive grants that need to be monitored. Usually, so many contacts are made during the course of the program that the grants administrator is guaranteed a huge, helpful, and powerful network.

The weekly *Chronicle of Higher Education,* published in Washington, also lists openings for instructors who have classroom experience in special education, accounting, educational materials, audio-visual techniques, and physical education. A master's degree is an advertised requirement, but even in these cases a bachelor's degree may be accepted if there is a convincing expertise offered. We often limit ourselves needlessly when it comes to requirements.

Educational Administrators in the Community

Not only colleges but women's centers, experimental schools, alternative schools, and the teacher training centers established to update teacher professionalism often have openings for administrators and teachers. The need for career education has stimulated the spread of career centers as more and more people seek career counseling. Such groups as Ys often conduct special education programs for men and women, and community agencies conduct support programs for widows, widowers, and the divorced. Wherever a workshop is advertised, some ambitious person has plunged into a study of the field and developed a curriculum that can be the basis for a new community offering—and a new career.

Is there a teachers' association or a branch office nearby? These associations have offices located throughout the state and frequently hire teachers for administrative positions. (Check the Yellow Pages of your telephone directory.)

Guidance centers, agencies new to the scene, have been created in some states to help students, counselors, and parents become better acquainted with employment opportunities and to foster a better understanding of career education. Seek them out, too.

Administration/Private Schools

Private elementary, secondary, and vocational-technical schools hire administrators to coordinate programs, plan curriculum, arrange conferences, place students in positions, and counsel students. Today, many specialized schools have been licensed to fill a specialized need, such as computer education. You could be hired as an Admissions Counselor or to do any of the above jobs. Visit a few local schools and read your newspapers for new situations that crop up continually. Don't reject the school because it is technical; technical schools hire many ex-teachers as administrators and as teachers, too.

After your having spent years in a classroom and having headed curriculum development groups, PTA functions, and other numerous community projects, administration may be just the thing for you.

The World of Nonprofit Is Profitable. If you can't find a job in one of the 40,000 nonprofit trade associations and professional societies in the United States, then you probably don't know where to look or haven't looked hard enough. (See the reference section of the Bibliography for sources of information.)

Let me make it clear to you that nonprofit does not mean that employees cannot earn money. Some large nonprofit associations bring in so much money that they have to find ways to give it away (in the form of scholarships, for instance). What it does mean is that the government has approved of these associations (and some companies, too, are included) because they are educational, conduct important research, and are in existence to foster professionalism or to further some consumer-related cause. These associations and companies pay their founders and executives very well, at the same time that they have excellent tax breaks. So don't let nonprofit associations and companies scare you away. As a matter of fact, these institutions favor former teachers because they are involved, very often, in educationally-related endeavors.

On the positive side is the news that associations may be one of the few havens left in the world unaffected by struggling economies. In fact, companies and agencies tend to lean on associations more heavily during a recession to find ways of improving their competitive edge.

Where do nonprofit associations obtain their recession-proof money? Members pay their way in the form of dues and entrance fees for conferences and lectures run by the association. There is a large enough membership, of course, to pay for the association's expenses.

Associations can be found in almost all fields, including teaching associations, as you well know. Examples of other fields are banking, medical, and consumer associations. Their function is to keep members informed of news and trends, act as spokespersons for related causes, conduct research, lobby, run conferences, and plan conventions.

Most associations need people with teaching ability for fund-raising, educational programming, and planning conventions and meetings. Just as in business, there are career opportunities in administration, public relations, marketing, advertising, and financial planning.

Associations reflect particular philosophies, so it makes sense to choose an association with a point of view that matches your own.

Salaries are commensurate with those in industry and keep up with inflation, but they top out around $100,000 for the very highest salary paid to the top executive in the country. (In industry, top executives can earn in the millions.)

As a teacher, would you settle for $100,000?

7. Sales Careers

When I was growing up in New York, there was an expression my father would use to describe someone who was good at getting a message across convincingly. "He could sell the Brooklyn Bridge to a stranger for $100," he would say.

In many ways teachers in the process of motivating students are selling them the Brooklyn Bridge. The same abilities, skills, and attitudes that are used to "sell" reading, English, and math are used to sell houses, business machines, a ticket to Honolulu, or a hundred shares of IBM. If teaching is no longer desirable, possible, or available, you should consider a career in sales.

Let's look at a few of the career fields that teachers have found well suited to their interests and abilities.

Manufacturer's Representative. A recent *Wall Street Journal* article reported that the average yearly salary of someone who has worked in a sales position for three years is $34,500. How does that sound to you? I think the figure is accurate, but it does not account for people who are above average, like teachers.

Once the domain of men, the sales force is being entered by

more and more women, especially those in need of a high income. These people sell a wide variety of products, from books to business machines, from electrical components to food products and drugs. Generally speaking, however, most sales items are those manufactured and then sold wholesale to hospitals, businesses, other manufacturers, schools, banks, and retail stores.

If you need a higher income, consider a sales job. All selling takes time to be successful, but the rewards can be worth the effort. And your bonuses need not be only financial ones; many former teachers find great enjoyment in working with adults as equals in the business world.

Though saleswork sometimes involves travel, not all your time will be spent selling. You will need to write reports, plan your work schedules, make appointments, bone up on the specifications for new products, and attend meetings. A woman once demonstrated a mini-computer to me. I happened to bump into her almost eighteen months later; she remembered not only where I worked but also my full name. Memory skills developed in teaching can boost a sales career.

Real Estate Sales. For those people seeking part- or full-time employment in their towns or nearby, real estate may be the answer. Requirements vary from state to state, but they usually entail some classroom training and a written test and are not difficult to fulfill. Knowledge of the neighborhood, towns, or cities you represent is important, however, because your clients will ask you about tax rates, churches, schools, public transportation, and many other matters. In most states real estate courses are given locally by either colleges or private firms.

The sale of commercial as opposed to residential properties is more lucrative because of the magnitude of the purchases, but an additional dimension of knowledge is necessary: for example, knowledge of business trends, leasing practices, availability of labor supply, and costs of different types of utilities for the particular area.

Employment opportunities in this field are excellent; Americans move frequently because of job transfers, and the number of people buying homes has been increasing sharply from year to year.

It is difficult to be successful in real estate if you do not stay on the job for at least a year. The sale of homes is seasonal, so you might not sell a home during October, November, or December but might sell several in April, May, June, and July.

Most beginning real estate agents work for a firm that is already established, in order to benefit from the training and resources available. Starting your own company or buying into a real estate franchise are also alternatives, however. Since laws vary between states, check the specific requirements to sell real estate in your state.

Insurance Sales. One teacher I knew could no longer afford to teach; he needed more money in order to educate his children. Research into the training programs of several major companies turned up an insurance company with an excellent reputation for producing salespeople who were knowledgeable and professional. This former English teacher intended to become a manager as soon as he learned the ins and outs of the insurance business. Using his motivational skills and enthusiasm, he was able to double his income. His high intelligence impressed not only former colleagues, who were delighted to seek advice from someone who had learned his new field thoroughly, but corporate officers with whom he did estate planning as well.

Another former teacher with a very different personality—low-key, soft-spoken, but still friendly and intelligent—has sold commerical insurance so successfully that he is semi-retiring at age fifty-two in order to spend more time in his three homes located in different parts of the world. In his quiet way, he has become successful because of the excellent service he provided and the trust he was able to inspire in his clients.

In order to sell insurance, you must obtain a license from the state in which you live. A written examination covering the insurance laws of the state and the fundamentals of writing insurance policies is usually mandatory. Training is done most often in the home office of the company, but previous business courses in accounting or finance can be extremely helpful.

The financial advantage of selling insurance comes from accumulating renewals from policies that are held from year to year. It is not uncommon to earn in the six figures after a few years.

The disadvantage of this job—if it is a disadvantage—is the work after hours that is necessary in order to close a deal. Women as well as men, however, have found this a very lucrative field.

Stock Broker. Although *stock broker* is the most common term for someone who deals in the purchase or sale of stock certificates, people who work in brokerage firms, insurance companies, or banks may also be called registered representatives, account executives, or customers' brokers. Brokerage firms, like the publishing industry, are now hiring more women, especially those who have been successful in another field.

After you receive a license (required by almost all states) you will be able to deal directly with customers. Training for the exam is usually provided by the company in both formal and observe-the-job styles.

If you have a flair for finance, economics, or even "wheeling and dealing," have a good reputation, speak effectively, and would enjoy the vicissitudes of the stock market, knock on the door of your nearest broker.

Advertising Salesperson. A young relative of mine graduated from college with a liberal arts degree and a handul of courses in elementary education. When he could not find a teaching job, he decided that he would use his verbal skills to sell advertisement air time for a local radio station. Within a year, Scott had earned $40,000—a success by any standard.

Although selling television time is more lucrative, selling advertising space in magazines and newspapers can bring in a fairly good income. At the same time, selling advertising space can expose you to a large number of businesspeople—a career education in itself and a possible source of future employment.

Travel Agent. What do teachers do on summer vacations and winter holidays? Frequently they travel. And when they are seeking jobs, they often think of a career in travel—that is, if they don't need much money, don't want to work full time, and do want to work near home. Unless you open your own agency, the travel business pays very poorly, not much more than minimum wages to start, although a clever person can insist on a small percentage of the business generated. But one teacher I know has opened her own business with a partner and still earns a good salary working part-time near her home.

Most travel agencies advertise for experienced people. Through an internship program, I have successfully placed adults in agencies where their complete training was done on the job. With a good sales talk you may convince an owner that you can learn on the job.

Many teachers I know have gone to special schools that train travel agents in the many details of this trade. If you are planning to attend, find a reputable school, preferably one that owns a few agencies, and ask for the names of several previous students. A telephone call or two will give you insight into the quality of the program and the placement possibilities.

Many people think that a travel agent's trips are all free of charge, a perk that goes with the job. This is, of course, untrue. Agents can receive discounts; and if you are lucky the owner might send you to a new hotel in Tahiti that is sponsoring a free "look-see" package. It does occur, but even owners love to travel—that's why they're in the business.

Owners or managers of travel agencies seek employees who have traveled and who are familiar with airlines, hotels, restaurants, and recreation facilties. Does this resemble anyone you know?

Automobile Salesperson. Years ago people made jokes about the lack of integrity of the used car salesman; that joke may soon be part of the nostalgia of the past.

A few years ago the recession hit the car industry. During that time many people patched their cars together instead of investing in new ones. In 1984 when the economy improved and cars started to look like patchwork quilts, the industry picked up speed. (Excuse the pun.)

Meanwhile, executives in the car industry had their ears tuned to market researchers who found out (1) that people who buy cars are more educated and sophisticated than ever before and (2) that today's computerized cars are more complex than ever. Conclusion?

Enter the educated salesperson. Heavily in demand, the nouveau style of salesperson is now being recruited on the college campus. It stands to reason that if a dealer wants to sell cars, he or she will have to cater to customers. And what the customer wants is a knowledgeable salesperson who knows the product and can talk the same language as the customer. The Ford Marketing Institute trains salespeople both in sales techniques and in the product. Car dealers have found that the new breed of salesperson stays on the job longer than most. And why not? A top salesperson can earn $50,000 selling Jaguars or Cadillacs. There is also the possibility of advancement into management or entry into one's own car dealership.

Dealers look for educated salespeople who are straightforward and HONEST—maybe a good start for a graduate and a career changer.

The joke about the used car salesman may soon be a myth.

Employment Agency Counselor or Recruiter. This job title is a new addition to the chapter on opportunities in sales. Since the first edition of this book appeared, I have opened my own employment agency, leaving the world of education behind me. If I may, I would like to share a personal experience with you, one that could help immeasurably with your own future.

When I was seeking an alternative career, I covered as many bases as possible. (See Chapter 13 for techniques.) I made an appointment at a private employment agency, where I learned several new lessons that affected my own professional life fortuitously. The first lesson was that teachers are rarely placed in industry by private employment agencies. The second lesson was that agencies serve as adjuncts to companies' own personnel departments. Recruiters in companies have a difficult time filling all their openings for experienced personnel, especially during times of fast economic growth. The third lesson I learned was that newspaper ads placed by companies rarely attract the most qualified candidates. Companies depend upon the agencies to search for and recruit highly qualified employees from among the competitors. (That is why agencies are called headhunters.)

The agency owner made it clear to me that I had come to the wrong place. If I wanted to get into industry, he couldn't help me; I would have to make my own effort because I did not have several years of relevant experience in a company. To my amazement, however, he offered me a job in his agency. I later found out that there were more than 3,000 agencies in the country that employed 50,000 counselors, many of whom had been teachers. So here is your opportunity.

But remember: this is a SALES position, not just employment counseling per se. You must sell your candidate's expertise to the company and sell the company's benefits to the candidate. If you can close the deal and "make the marriage," as they say, you can make money. This is a people-oriented business for those who are comfortable on the telephone, enjoy meeting candidates and officers in companies, and can write a convincing cover letters and resumes for candidates.

Counselors also use the agency route to enter personnel departments in industry. After all, every day in an agency you speak to managers and presidents of companies and become professional friends with many. You are one of the first people to hear about new job openings in their companies before they hit the papers. In fact, after I started my own business, I helped one former teacher to reach his greatly desired goal of entering industry. I recruited him from an agency and placed him with a manufacturing company as a recruiter. His last remarks to me were, "Why didn't I do this earlier? I'm so happy. I love it." Needless to say, he is also happy to hire good candidates I present to the company!

Recruiting is a wonderful people-oriented sales business where a talented counselor can earn from $25,000 to $100,000 a year—and more. In this business it is possible to go through a training program, especially in the larger companies or franchises. Former teachers have also become trainers in employment agencies.

Are you starting to get the idea that former teachers are everywhere?

8. Self-Employment

Many people speak about the era in which we live as the "me generation," meaning that people nowadays are predominantly egocentric. Perhaps disillusionment with government and institutions and the resulting desire to "do my own thing" have been the catalysts for the recent proliferation of self-owned businesses.

What are the advantages of owning your own business? The obvious response is that you won't have to look for a job or please a boss. You can use your talents on your own behalf. Although most entrepreneurs work seven days and nights a week in order to get the show on the road, your goal may be to establish flexible work hours or an alternative life style—sleeping late or working at home. Many successful people do operate out of their homes, at least in the beginning. Some giant corporations in existence today began in a basement or a garage. Your business may be so successful that you can use it as collateral for a loan—to start another business! For entrepreneurs, this is not at all uncommon.

Statistics are against the success of most new businesses,

actually. Twenty percent fail in the first year; fifty percent fail in the second. But Americans are risk takers; most entrepreneurs either don't know the statistics or decide to defy them.

There are approximately 13 million small businesses in the country. A small business is defined as one that has from one to five hundred people; they generate more jobs than any other sector. In 1983, however, there was a record of almost 29,000 failures. The expression may be trite, but it has been echoed by many entrepreneurs: "Better to have tried and lost than never to have tried at all." These were my father's sentiments after his business failed. In typical entrepreneurial style, however, he started an entirely different business and worked at it until he retired at age 72.

Another age-old conundrum is the question, "Are entrepreneurs born or made?" Many studies have examined this question, but results are always inconclusive because creativity—necessary in any start-up venture—is elusive and therefore difficult to measure. My own experience tells me that there is a combination of "born" and "made" factors, with an emphasis on the "made" (or skill) side.

Before I continue with self-employment in general, I would like to ask your indulgence in continuing the story begun in the last chapter, in order to provide you with further insights into my own thought process after I was offered a job in the employment agency business; you may benefit from my experience.

My own success story: Sandy Pollack Associates, Inc. I left the agency on that day quite stunned; sparks of emotion and streams of ideas, most of which had nothing to do with accepting the job offer, vied successively in my brain.

Friends, co-workers, family—people who knew me well— had for years been telling me that I was an entrepreneurial type. I had been asked time and time again, "How come you don't start your own business?" Often I had become angry at their questions because my own goals did not include starting a business of my own—again. (To be honest with you, I must admit that I had already started a small business, which I terminated.) But that day was different. I was really excited because I knew instinctively that an employment agency would fit my experience, skills, and personal need for autonomy and flexibility.

I began immediately to inquire into the expenses associated with the business and was relieved to discover that the costs were not prohibitive. Within four weeks I left my college position, rented and furnished two offices, hired my secretary (Therese had already worked for me at the college and is still with me after three years), and set about trying to learn a business I had not worked in previously.

All employees do some on-the-job training, and I was no exception. I had to devise all the office procedures, write my own advertisements for candidates, introduce myself and the company to hundreds of high-tech companies, learn the jargon of the business, and, last but not least, pay all the bills, which accumulated rapidly. And all of this during a recession, which hit many businesses heavily! (Maybe I was lucky, because half my competitors went out of business in 1982, my first year in business.)

I worked hard, used every contact I could (my network), and was surprised to find the company profitable at the end of its first year.

Now that my business is three years old and I've incorporated, I have to admit that my family, friends, and co-workers were right; I am a classic entrepreneur: self-motivated, creative, confident in my abilities, independent, and risk-oriented. (Test your own skills and attributes on the checklist that follows.) Who knows? Although I love the business, maybe this will not be my last one or only one, either. And maybe you, too, will be successful in starting a business of your own.

Tips on Getting Started

Where does the former teacher, now inspired to be an entrepreneur, begin? Only you can actually decide on the enterprise that suits you best. Chances are you have already toyed with two or three ideas. If you still need inspiration, see the list at the end of this chapter. But there is more to starting a business than just printing up a business card and stationery. Most businesses fail because of poor management, and often insufficient time is allotted to the planning stages. Here is a bare-bones outline of steps to take.

Research. First, gather information. If you are so inclined, get a master's degree in business or enroll in a business college and take courses in accounting, marketing, and the like. Interview as many professionals in your proposed field as you can. You will be pleased to find that many professionals are willing to advise the neophyte. If you are offered a job, take it, if you have the time. Is there a better way to gain inside information? Many newly-formed companies are spinoffs from other firms. (In some ways, I wish I had done this first; I could have saved time and money by learning the business from pros.)

In your planning stage, join a trade association or a business-person's group. Information and contacts made there can have a future payoff, and the success stories of others will be stimulating.

Next, determine the size of the budget you will need for the first six months or the first year. Estimate the length of time it will take you to earn some profit—this is called start up time. Plan a budget that includes such things as rent, supplies, advertising, telephones, electricity, secretarial help, insurance, gas, printing, heat, mailings, interest on loans, and legal fees. Then increase this figure by fifty percent—and make sure the money is completely available before you start. (You'll need more than you think.)

Consider where you will locate your business. Does your place of business have to be visible to the public? Is accessibility important? A real estate agent will be helpful in scouting out places. Your local newspaper can help, too.

Does the community or industry need your kind of business? A market survey can tell whether your new boutique or bookstore is needed in the area you have in mind. Stop people on the street and ask them. Send out a trial mailing or call people, using your telephone directory. Or employ a market research firm—specialists in the field—to do this work for you.

Research the markets (people, stores, companies, industries, and so on) where your items can be used. Do you have a sales and distribution plan? You may have intriguing products to sell,

but you cannot make money if no one hears about them. What kind of advertising have you planned in your budget? How much time will you have for advance and general public relations? Attending community and organizational meetings is effective, but it takes time. Word of mouth takes time, too. Seek out answers while you are conducting your investigation.

Funding. Find out where to apply for funds. Using up all your savings is a bad idea. You will probably be stingy about spending money and will feel insecure. Talk to your local banker about a loan *after* you have taken the above steps. A friend can help you to prepare a pro forma balance sheet (a written business plan estimating expenses and projected income for about a six-month period). With luck, your preparation and knowledge will impress your banker.

The federal Small Business Administration (SBA) is mandated to assist women and minorities as well as other individuals desiring to go into business. The advantage in dealing with the SBA is that it provides a very important service—management assistance—*free of charge.* This service could save you hundreds, maybe thousands, of dollars. The government also sets aside contracts specifically for small businesses to bid on, in order to encourage such businesses.

Another possible source of starting capital is a Small Business Investment Company (SBIC). The government has helped create such companies, but they are not well known. You should know in advance that these companies, if they invest in your business, own a part of it and have a voice in its operations. Some entrepreneurs see this as an advantage; others want to go it alone.

Individuals and groups who invest in new business ventures are called venture capitalists. If you have a good business in mind and you look like a good risk, they may invest in your business. But don't be surprised if they too put their toes in your door. Leads to these individuals may be available through your local Chamber of Commerce (a good source of information about local businesses), your bank, your local financial newspaper, your lawyer, or the SBA.

Don't rush to start your business. Finding out about it first can lead to future rewards. Much of your learning will take place on the job, but the extra planning time that you take will help you avoid many headaches.

Think Big. One of the pitfalls of planning a new venture is thinking too small. In other words, you say, "What's the least I need to open my travel agency?" That can be a mistake. Why think small when you can think big? Your goal may be to remain a small business, but if you start out with insufficient funds you may not even get the business off the ground. Remember, it takes time to build an established business. Why not try to arrange a bigger loan, over a longer period of time, that will allow you the time and the maneuverability to flourish and succeed? Further, the sources of capital will be more receptive to a plan that demonstrates sound thinking. They will turn down a plan whose budget is too low, if it is unrealistic.

Partners. Although a partnership arrangement has its advantages, I made the decision to go it alone in my own business. I was influenced by a businessman who told me that he was unhappy with his own partner. He advised me in this manner: "If you take a partner, grow to dislike each other, and decide to dissolve the partnership, you create a lot of animosity, hardship, and emotional trauma. On the other hand, if you hire someone who doesn't live up to your standards, you can always fire the person."

Since I recently found it necessary to fire an employee for lack of performance, I am happy that I took Bill's advice. Firing an employee is difficult enough; breaking up a partnership is traumatic.

For you, starting a business with a trusted friend or associate may be helpful, especially with problem-solving. Perhaps the person you have in mind will complement your talents by concentrating on one particular facet of the business. A partner on your team can serve as a catalyst to spur you on when your energy level is low; there is no doubt that two of the right heads are better than one, and certainly four hands can accomplish more than two.

Success story: an educational materials business. Dedicated teachers love their students well enough to spend their own hard-earned salaries on educational materials, which they use in their classrooms. They can spend $50 to $100 when they see puzzles and games that they know will excite their students. This money is not refunded by their school systems.

In Lexington, Massachusetts, my home town, a former teacher started his own retail store, School's Inn, dedicating himself to offering teachers educational materials that would provide the best price break he could manage.

Teachers make many purchases for their pupils and love to buy the Laurie puzzles and the International Playthings puzzles and toys, among other things. Parents come in droves at Christmas and birthday time. The store caters to everyone from babies to parents, who buy computer business software, a newly-added product.

All the materials sold in the store have an educational flavor. Customers are served by former teachers who have taught art, English, history and music, so you can't find a better-trained sales force anywhere!

In order to serve a broader public, the company printed a catalog that is sent to schools in many states. And just to indicate how businesslike they are, salespeople—teachers, of course—travel to neighboring states to familiarize principals with exciting materials that are available in hopes that they will make purchases.

Schools' Inn is not unique. There are similar companies operating under other names (Hammett's, for instance) in other localities like California, Rhode Island, Vermont, New Hampshire, and Maine. There is even an association called ESANE that has sprung up to serve this market. (See the Appendix.) The association officers—teachers, naturally—give workshops on marketing and business subjects and publish a directory of resources for teachers. There are about 400 former teachers who belong to this association; most of them are salespeople.

Have you heard enough? Did you know that so many teachers were at the head of their classes?

Which Kind of Business? The business you decide to start should suit the person you are today. That is to say, the business should mesh with your current interests, personality, and skills. Don't make the common mistake of selecting an interest that amused you at age sixteen, unless you are still intrigued with the idea and still suited to the business. If you weighed just over a hundred pounds at age sixteen, opening a modeling agency might have been appropriate, but if you tip the scales at two hundred today, unless you gear the business to the oversized you may be making a mistake. Test your fantasies with a heavy dose of realism.

Many career changers plunge into entirely new waters, ones that reflect their new visions; motivation can reap wonders. Farmers have become physicians, physicians have become real estate tycoons, engineers have become lawyers—and teachers have become all of these. What was their motivation? Anything from the desire to make money through the desire for a part-time work schedule that would accommodate family needs.

A part-time business of one's own is becoming more and more popular today, especially as women born in the baby boom start their own families. Business does offer excellent part-time opportunities as well as the benefit of being able to deduct the cost of babysitters and a percentage of all business-related expenses. Known as consultants, many former teachers are involved in part-time sales, word processing, publishing, computer programming, advertising, and decorating, to name several businesses.

In my opinion, many teachers will succeed at business because they have transferrable skills. Haven't they already succeeded in running a mini-business, the classroom? Add to their former successes a measure of business skills—and luck—and we'll be reading about them in *Fortune* magazine.

Here are some other possibilities for businesses you may start:

Accounting firm	Cheese and gourmet shop
Advertising consultant	Collection agency
Antique shop	Commercial art studio
Art gallery or rental	Computer Store
Babysitting agency	Convalescent home
Beauty salon	Convention coordinator
Book publisher; bookstore	Copy and printing service
Bride and groom clothing shop	Dancing and music school
Bridge-teaching studio	Decorator service (business or
Burglar alarm company	home)
Catering	Drapery and fabric shop

Employment counselor
Employment agency
Escort service
Fashion boutique
Flower and plant shop
Gift and card shop
Handbags/totes (wholesale)
Health food store
Insurance agency
Jewelry store
Knit and wool store
Leasing equipment agency
Literary agency
Mail-order business
Manufacturer
Manufacturer's representative
Market research
Newsletter company
Newspaper publisher

Paperback bookshop
Party store
Personal shopper or errand agency
Photographer
Pottery and china shop
Public relations consultant
Real estate agency
Restaurant
Remedial reading consultant
Secretarial service
Small business consultant
Telephoning answering service
Training consultant for industry
Translating agency
Travel agency
Venture capital business
Weight loss salon
Wine shop

If the idea of owning a business hasn't stimulated you into action yet, then either you haven't enough information to form an opinion (if this is so, see the Bibliography) or business is not a viable route for you (take the test that follows, to judge for yourself).

As president of my own small corporation, I have met all my professional and personal objectives. Ask yourself, "Has the time for my own business arrived?"

Test Your Entrepreneurial Skills

	Yes	No
Self-motivated	☐	☐
Creative	☐	☐
Persistent	☐	☐
Confident	☐	☐
Willing to keep learning	☐	☐
Flexible	☐	☐
Independent	☐	☐
Empathetic	☐	☐
Excellent communication skills	☐	☐
Systems oriented	☐	☐
Problem-solver	☐	☐
Decisive	☐	☐
Resourceful	☐	☐
Disciplined	☐	☐
Accept risks	☐	☐
Optimistic	☐	☐
Capable	☐	☐
Persuasive	☐	☐
Financially set for one year	☐	☐
Energetic	☐	☐
Enthusiastic	☐	☐

9. Working
For the Government

The government is a big employer. Towns, cities, states, and the federal government pay the salaries of one out of every five working people. Despite the fact that administrators are cutting budgets, there will always be professional jobs because of the need for replacements due to retirement, relocation, expansion in specific departments, and other reasons.

Teachers used to shy away from bureaucracies, but recent exposure to school politics has inured them to institutional life and prepared them for entry into government and business· careers. In government there are jobs for educators and administrators that offer excellent salaries from $20,000 upwards.

Even though seeking a job in government appears to be overwhelming to the uninitiated, the procedure is not as difficult as you may think. Your first step is to locate the personnel department in your town, city, state, or federal agency. (Federal agencies have branch offices, too, throughout the United States.) Look in the Yellow Pages of your telephone directory under *Government* and then seek the particular category: County, Town,

City, State, U. S., or Civil Service Commission. Don't attempt to do a survey on the telephone, because government office lines are always busy and besides employees cannot possibly convey to you, on the telephone, all the available job information.

When you visit the employment office, be prepared to spend several hours. After you read the job descriptions you may want to fill out the relevant applications. Since government applications are lengthy and detailed, make certain you bring a current resume or an up-to-date fact sheet that covers your life from the cradle to your current status. If you were born outside the United States, you may also need proof of citizenship.

Frequently, the state and the federal government have jobs of a civilian nature. Examples of civilian jobs are teacher, librarian, and counselor, all of whom may be needed to work at a local air base, for instance; inquire about the many civilian jobs that are open.

The government often requires tests in order to qualify a person for certain positions; this information will be made available to you when you make an application. Tests are administered on specific dates and are scheduled in advance, so you must be certain to ask for this information if it is not proffered.

The advantage of listing with a government agency, according to the Department of Labor statistics, is the smaller number of applicants for each federal job. An average of 250 people apply for a job in the private sector, through ads placed in the Sunday employment section of newspapers—a much higher number than those for the public sector. Most government jobs never reach the newsstands; they are listed with the personnel department of the government office. Here's how the system works.

The state civil service commission, for example, has a resume bank. When a job opening occurs, a few resumes are selected and sent to the government agency requesting the resumes. If you are registered, have good qualifications, and made good test scores, you will get that most-sought-after commodity, the interview. With just three or so resumes in the agency's hands (instead of the 250 responses from newspaper ads), you are more likely to receive a job offer.

There are also some jobs that require no tests in advance.

These are called provisional; in other words, you can get the job on the provision that you take the exam when it is given.

Where to Look

State Departments of Education. There are 55 state departments of education and 70 federal agencies supporting education. Regional and local offices are scattered throughout the states; there may be one very close to your home.

In addition, the United States Office of Education serves as liaison between federal and state educational programs that involve colleges, professional associations, and international educational organizations. A bachelor's degree is an acceptable degree for most of the following jobs, although a master's degree is preferred:

- Administration
- Research
- Consulting
- Career Program Director
- Career Specialist
- Educational Program Assistant
- Curriculum Specialist
- Handicapped Specialist

Employment Services: Division of Employment Security. There are 2,500 state employment offices in the United States, where the unemployed pick up their checks and seek employment. These offices provide counseling, testing, placement, and referral, as well as listings of available positions. If you register with the state Civil Service Commission, you could be employed by the employment office, too. One former teacher worked at such a job and then moved on to an administrative position in private industry that he found by "being in the employment system and knowing where the jobs were." Many companies list their openings with the DES.

Joint Programs: Government and Business. In 1983 the government replaced CETA (a job training program insufficiently effective in retraining and permanently placing the unemployed) with the Job Training Partnership Act, a $3.5 billion program to retrain and place the unemployed. The design of the program has resulted from an innovative, collaborative effort between industry and government. PICs (Private Industry Councils) is the acronym by which the business groups are known. The Employment and Training Administration oversees the training, and the private sector supplies on-the-job training and jobs. Groups targeted to receive training are disadvantaged adults and youths and workers displaced by technological obsolescence. Since forty percent of the funds have been allocated to train sixteen- to twenty-one-year-olds, high school teachers who have been laid off or who seek part-time teaching assignments may be able to qualify for teaching positions in this program.

Because a millon people will be trained annually in this program, there may be an opportunity for you to add your expertise or to develop a new skill. In this program, many types of training are taking place: accounting, secretarial, basic subjects, and others. In all parts of the program, people are needed to handle the personnel problems, to counsel, to design and administer the curriculum, to serve as liaison with the companies, to work in public relations, to write, and to replace people who leave.

To locate the program in your vicinity, inquire at your local Divison of Employment Security (see the Yellow Pages of your telephone directory under your particular state offices); the DES is the intake center for the program. (An intake center identifies the people who need retraining.) Odd as it may seem, if you are unemployed, you may yourself qualify for retraining! In Bedford, Massachusetts, Middlesex Community College has a subsidized Technical Writing program for unemployed teachers. You should call your local urban colleges to locate retraining programs; many former teachers have successfully taken this route. Remember, too, that your local Chamber of Commerce knows of the programs that are in existence in your area.

Career Titles to Explore

Commissioner. Important-sounding titles are often used in government positions to describe department heads. An example is Commissioner of Education, or Affirmative Action Commissioner.

The job is obtained by scoring high on a civil service exam. In order to comply with the federal mandate to provide management jobs for women, government agencies have placed women in these positions. (Of course, men are welcome to apply, too.)

Compliance Officer. If you are on civil service lists, you are eligible for this position. A compliance officer checks up on companies that do business with the government to ensure that they comply with government regulations for hiring minorities.

Because you are required to make on-site visits to companies, you will have the exciting opportunity of dealing with presidents of companies. You can see that your network could soon be burgeoning with influential people.

In this position, minorities may receive preferential treatment. Salaries are in the $18,000 to $20,000 range.

Job Developer. A job developer finds employment for specific individuals by reaching out into local companies. A handicapped programmer may need to find a job in the community, for instance. The job developer's responsibility would be to call companies in the area to urge them to hire the programmer. Counseling of applicants is part of this job, as is constant contact with personnel departments in all types of businesses. Job development is well suited to teachers.

Since most job development work is done through state and federal programs, it is necessary to file papers with both types of personnel managers in order to be eligible for employment.

Legislative Assistant. This position is difficult to find on the federal or state level without a law degree, but can be found, although not readily, on the town, county, or city level.

An assistant helps a legislator with all the duties of the office, including statistical analysis, research, public relations, campaigning, coordinating projects, dealing with constituents, office management, lobbying, liaison with other agencies, writing reports, interviewing, maintaining media contact, attending social functions, and keeping records. The job calls for reading, writing, and communicating—all skills associated with teaching—as well as organizing, coordinating, planning, and executing projects.

Political aficionados may have the best luck in obtaining this job if they have supported the legislator in the past.

Volunteer for an ACTION Job

If you have "had it up to here" with administration or early morning rush hour, or are ready for retirement, you may be ready for a volunteer position of your choice. (Volunteering can also be excellent for networking.)

In addition to volunteer opportunities in your own community, ACTION, the government's broadly inclusive volunteer agency, has many organized programs in which your services would be welcome. Some of these programs provide volunteers with a modest tax-free stipend, a transportation allowance, a hot meal when possible, insurance, and an annual physical exam.

You may never have heard of ACTION, but nearly 326,000 people have already paved the way for you; several thousand new people join ACTION programs each year, forty-five percent males and fifty-five percent females of all ages.

Several of the ACTION programs are listed below. For more information, call (800) 424–8580.

VISTA: Volunteers in Service to America. More than 70,000 VISTA volunteers have worked with the poor of America (approximately 25 million people) teaching them how to help themselves to improve their situations. Volunteers assigned for one- or two-year terms have been politically influential in obtaining beneficial legislation for their groups. People who volunteer for these programs come from all walks of life and choose the settings in which they want to work. They may select to work in an urban or a rural setting, in their own community (seventy percent do this), on an Indian reservation, or wherever they are needed. VISTA volunteers may work on cases of drug abuse, in health programs, in education, or on any community issue. Call the ACTION number listed above to receive a booklet entitled VISTA that may inspire you to act; volunteer programs have changed the direction of people's careers.

Other ACTION Programs. You should keep in mind that ACTION runs other programs as well that advertise for paid help from time to time. All these programs use paid teachers, administrators, counselors, and volunteers. To be eligible it is important to get on the federal job listings; people are called up from these lists.

Call the toll-free number for ACTION listed above to obtain addresses for the following programs.

ADPP: ACTION Drug Prevention Program. ADPP works to support local and national efforts to help young people remain drug-free. ADPP works in conjunction with corporate and business leaders, so working with groups like this provides good networking for job-seekers.

NCSL: National Center for Service Learning. NCSL is a program that provides technical assistance, materials, training seminars, research, and on-site consultation to local college and high schools.

OVL: Office of Volunteer Liaison. OVL provides a link between ACTION and private volunteer programs in the United States and abroad.

RSVP: Retired Senior Volunteer Program. RSVP offers older citizens the opportunity to use their talents and experience in community service. For teachers, this is a boon, because they can tutor or teach if they desire. There is no stipend, but transportation costs may be obtainable. The possibility for travel exists, too, because RSVP volunteers serve in 728 different projects in all fifty states and in Puerto Rico, the Virgin Islands, and Guam.

YVA: Young Volunteers in ACTION. YVA is a nationwide corps of volunteers age fourteen to twenty-two who serve their communities. Volunteers serve on a part-time basis at least eight hours per month.

The Peace Corps. If you can make a strong commitment to people in need, can learn their language, adapt to their customs, help them to start small businesses, show them how to farm their land economically, aid them in building schools, and assist them in educating both children and adults, you may be eligible to become a volunteer in the Peace Corps.

Started in 1961 by President John F. Kennedy and his brother, Robert, the corps has graduated more than a hundred thousand volunteers who have served in sixty-four countries, primarily in Africa, Latin America, Central America, and other developing nations. Volunteers come from almost every state: Massachusetts, New York, Pennsylvania, Michigan, and California have sent the majority. Many have taken intensive training in any of 114 languages and dialects. Skill is the name of the game in the new Peace Corps philosophy.

The Corps seeks teachers, tradespeople, farmers, business-people, engineers, nurses, home economists, nutritionists, and math and science majors. Each volunteer is matched up with the particular needs of the requesting countries. If you join, for your service you will receive a minimum allowance from the time your training begins and $175 for every month of service after your contract has expired.

Volunteers learn to eat pounded plantains in Cameroon or manioc leaves and squash seeds in Zaire. They are also trained in native customs and learn that in the country they will be living in it may be an affront to shake hands or to touch someone with the left hand. They are involved in the constructing of solar projects, the creation of fish ponds, and the education of the entire community.

A profile of volunteers in the Peace Corps looks like this:

Average age   28.5 years
Men   53 percent
Women   47 percent
Married (no children permitted)   15 percent
Minorities   6 percent
Older Americans   6.5 percent
    (Very desirable, especially if they have been in business or in a trade)
U.S. Citizens   100 percent

The Peace Corps is definitely not for the weak-minded, and although people are carefully screened and trained, 27 percent of volunteers terminate their contracts before the committed two-year period. (Interestingly, 14 percent *extend* their contracts.) Obviously, the government feels that the Peace Corps volunteer serves an outstanding purpose in helping poor countries, because $29,000 is spent on each volunteer each year to prepare and support them in every way possible. The 1983 total allocation was $108.5 million dollars for 5,200 volunteers. Other people must think that the program is worthwhile, too, because the state of Connecticut, for example, permits public school teachers to serve for two years in the Peace Corps, and Massachusetts is considering doing this, too; Columbia University gives graduate credits for Peace Corps service.

Thousands of requests for volunteers are received by the Peace Corps from participating countries. The following job description is a typical example:

Requirements: B.A./B.S. in home economics or nutrition; with or without experience.

Prefer: Ability to sew

As a *Home Economics Teacher* in the Peace Corps your assignment will vary depending on the country and project in which you may be asked to serve. You may be working with the Ministry of Education in the planning, implementation, and evaluation of home economics programs; providing in-service teacher training, developing adequate resource and technical materials as needed; giving workshops and seminars. You may be assigned to a teacher-training institute, a secondary school, or an extension center providing needed expertise in needlework, sewing, home management, cooking, and food hygiene. Or, you may be teaching high schools on a regular basis giving students and teachers a background in the many facets of home economics. In all cases, you will be involved in the daily life of your local community, whether you are giving nutrition seminars to community groups or organizing such secondary activities as school and home gardens, adult education, youth groups, sports, music, etc.

Housing will be modest, perhaps lacking electricity, running water, stoves, and refrigeration. You may live alone, with another volunteer, or with a host country family.

Training will usually be held in the country of assignment and will vary from eight to twelve weeks in length. It will include intensive language training, cross-cultural studies, and a technical orientation to your assignment.

Final placement will be made by the Peace Corps Office of Volunteer Placement in Washington D.C., taking into account your geographic and assignment preferences. However, priority will continue to be given to the specific needs of the various countries requesting volunteers.

Volunteering is in favor today, perhaps as a beneficial effect of a good economy, the support of the president of the United States, and the caring attitude of a mature society that has lived through the pain of the sixties and seventies—a visible sign that we are recovering emotionally.

10. Alternative Careers: More Options To Consider

The careers described in this chapter vary widely. I have included some of them because teachers have expressed interest in hearing about a full range of options in order to satisfy their thirst for career education. Many of these careers can be sought by teachers as viable alternatives at salaries commensurate with or higher than the wages of a teacher. Others may be considered entry-level jobs. Remember, an entry-level job can be a steppingstone to an entirely new world.

What is an entry-level job? It is one on the lowest rung of a career ladder. A position as an expediter for instance, could lead to a position as a purchasing agent—a very well-paid job available in hospitals, industry, business, and government. A position as an employment interviewer could lead to a job as a personnel manager. As you acquire more proficiency and confidence, you can climb the ladder to more prestigious positions. Remember that from seventy to eighty percent of job openings never hit the newspapers; they are filled within the company. Isn't that a good reason to work hard to find a new career even at an entry level? You, too, can rise to greater heights after you join the system.

In the list of alternative careers below, I have included positions that are above entry-level in order to present a broader career picture. Teachers have been very successful in making rapid progress up the ladder.

Accountant.* To facilitate executive decisions, managers rely on accountants for the preparation and analysis of their financial data. Within the three major accounting fields—public, management, and government—there are many opportunities for specialization. Public accountants may concentrate on auditing or tax matters; management consultants may advise industry on.effective accounting systems; government accountants may work as Internal Revenue agents or bank examiners.

Although smaller accounting firms will hire graduates from business colleges, larger public accounting and business firms require a B.A. in either accounting or a related field, or they give preference to those with a master's degree in accounting. Certified Public Accountants (C.P.A.s) hold a certificate issued by the state; in most states you must complete a minimum of two years of field work before you can apply for certification.

Before considering an accounting career, you should be certain you have an aptitude for mathematics as well as the ability to handle responsibility and to work independently.

Opportunities are abundant for part-time work, particularly in smaller firms; if you want to enroll in a graduate program, you can still support yourself in this occupation. Average salaries start at $20,000.

Actuary. Why do young persons pay more for auto insurance than older persons? How much should an insurance policy cost?

Answers to these and similar questions are provided by actuaries who work for insurance companies. In order to answer

---

*Most of the careers listed here have been adapted from the *Occupational Outlook Handbook.*

these questions, they must keep abreast of economic, social and medical trends, and analyze statistics and data.

If you have a B.A. degree and have majored in mathematics or have taken a statistics course, you can qualify for this position in one of the nation's fastest-growing fields. First, however, you must evaluate your potential as an actuary. There are three societies that administer tests: (1) the Society of Actuaries, (2) the Casualty Actuarial Society, and (3) the American Society of Pension Actuaries.

Beginners in this field prepare tabulations of calculations used in insurance reports. With experience, you may aspire to administrative positions all the way to the top of the company, where an executive can earn $50,000 or more.

Affirmative Action Officer or Equal Employment Opportunity (E.E.O) Specialist. Any institution with fifteen or more employees must appoint an affirmative action officer, who is to hire minorities and handicapped persons and to compile and report hiring statistics relating to them. Large companies may hire several people in this capacity. The E.E.O. specialist's job is to foster positive attitudes between supervisors and other managers, set up grievance procedures, do creative problem-solving, and implement training programs that provide upward mobility.

This position is well suited to teachers who are qualified for entry-level jobs as assistants to E.E.O. specialists; minorities may have an employment advantage.

Administrative Assistant. Don't be fooled by this job title: it is rarely a management position. It is simply an elegant way of describing the work of an intelligent, preferably educated, secretary who types, takes shorthand, is reliable, and manages the office better than the boss could ever do. But it is a door opener.

Political officials do, however, use administrative assistants, in a managerial sense, to carry out the many projects within their domain. If you are active politically, you may be in a position to seek this political plum, which legislators and other government officials bestow on their loyal helpers.

Teachers are accepting positions as administrative assistants after taking crash programs in office management at private business schools. This route can lead them into an immediate job, because educated secretaries are in high demand. Let me emphasize: this is a great steppingstone and has led to huge successes.

If you enter this field, when you finish your studies you should sign up with a temporary employment agency. Several short-term assignments from three to six months' duration will provide you with an all-expenses-paid opportunity to learn about the business world. Each company is unique and has its own culture and personality. If you are observant, you will find positions and opportunities you never knew existed. Choose your place of employment carefully and seize opportunities for more responsibilities—and more money! An ex–French teacher became Assistant to the Dean of Faculty within one year by selecting her job carefully and keeping her goal in mind.

The job will call for skills that many teachers possess: coordinating the activities of an office, interviewing and advertising for jobs, preparing a budget, conducting management studies, and planning training programs.

Top salaries for administrative assistants are from $25,000 to $30,000 for the experienced.

Banking Careers. There's more to banking than being a teller.

Because banks have radically expanded the services they offer to the community, opportunities will proliferate in this fast-growing business.

Banks usually have training programs in which new employees are trained in banking practices. Candidates may be placed as loan or trust officers (lending money or investing money for individuals and companies), as systems analysts (to devise better procedures for the paper flow), as branch managers, in personnel, and in public relations departments. Educational requirements vary from the B.A. to the M.B.A. degrees.

Many teachers have made exciting transitions into banking. One former teacher loves her position in public relations, where there is heavy community contact, a practice to which banks are committed. Another ex-teacher is delighted working as a loan officer, where she works with company presidents. Remember, banks have large training departments, too, where employees receive training in clerical skills, English, and management. Banks use curriculum developers and other writers to develop their workshop materials.

If you plan on entering this industry, where beginning salaries range from $16,000 to $30,000, make certain that your economics and finance courses are recent. You may wish to contact the American Bankers Association, located in twelve areas throughout the country, for details and requirements in the banking industry. This association trains officers in different specialties. The ABA, Bank Personnel Division, is located at 1120 Connecticut Avenue N.W., Washington, DC 20036.

They say that if you like money, you'll like banking.

Bookkeeper. Every business operation needs to maintain systematic and up-to-date records of its accounts and business transactions. In small firms, the general bookkeeper analyzes and records all financial transactions, balances the accounts, and handles the payroll.

Bookkeeping positions are available in all kinds of firms, especially in wholesale and retail trade. In addition, factories, banks, insurance companies, hospitals, and schools all hire a certain number of bookkeepers to manage their records.

If you have had any training in business math, accounting, or bookkeeping, whether in high school or college, you are eligible for a bookkeeping position.

To begin with, you need an above-average aptitude for working with numbers, ability to concentrate on detail, and willingness to work as part of a team. Often the bookkeeping experience, along with some accounting courses, can be your entree into the accounting field.

Thousands of job openings in this field will be available every year over the next decade; computer knowledge is desirable.

Collection Agent. When customers do not pay their bills, their accounts are often turned over to a private company that will attempt to obtain the overdue funds. This is a very lucrative field for those who can successfully arrange a method of payment with the client. Jobs are available, pay very well, and are suited to teachers with good verbal skills.

Coordinator. Wherever there is a program to be organized and managed, the services of a coordinator will be needed. Examples of a coordinator's position are a speaker's bureau coordinator, an out-patient coordinator, and an out-of-state visitor's coordinator. Skills required are all within the range of teachers: good communication, ability to organize, and interpersonal skills; salaries are commensurate with or higher than those for teachers.

Look for coordinating positions in colleges, social service agencies, government, hospitals, business, and apartment complexes. (When I worked at a college, I coordinated the college's speakers' bureau.)

Counselor. There are many places and environments within which a counselor may function. All schools from elementary school through college employ counselors, as do state, private, or community agencies. School counselors, the largest group by far, help students with their personal, social, and educational development. Employment counselors work in state offices, various private and community agencies, prisons, training schools, and mental hospitals where they counsel the unemployed or unskilled in job and career choices. Rehabilition counselors help people with mental, physical, or emotional disabilities to become self-sufficient and productive citizens. Some counselors teach in graduate training programs or conduct research.

For most counseling positions, either a master's degree in counseling or some graduate courses are necessary. Volunteer counseling or teaching can sometimes substitute for course work for an entry-level position. (Check your state for particular requirements.) Employment counselors who work in private agencies sometimes have no degree, but work experience is required. A student may find employment during the summer in employment agencies even before obtaining a degree. Internships in counseling are extremely valuable because they provide hands-on experience, an advantage when seeking employment.

Curriculum Developer. Teachers who have already worked on committees to develop classroom curricula can use this experience to obtain positions with private research companies, educational departments in government agencies, banks, nonprofit educational firms, educational materials companies, or educational associations (see Chapter 6).

If curriculum development interests you, attend a meeting of the American Society for Curriculum Development. A master's degree is desirable but experience in a particular subject is acceptable. If you have some particular expertise, go out and market your skills, because they are valuable.

Banks and business firms use curriculum developers to create courses that can be used in house. English programs, English as a second language courses, business letter and report-writing programs, and business skill courses all fall into this category. Salaries start at about $20,000.

Customer Service Representative. This is an entry-level position into many businesses that requires an ability to work well with people. In industry, the customer service representative deals with customers in order to help solve any problems they have concerning deliveries and orders. He or she works with other employees throughout the company in an attempt to determine the progress or the whereabouts of a customer's order.

Most teachers possess the skills needed to qualify for this position—tact, good oral skills, problem-solving ability, letter-composing skill, interpersonal skills, and patience. From this position you can go to many spots in a company—personnel, sales, marketing, public relations, training, customer service, or wherever your skills and interest take you.

Development/Fundraising. Colleges, universities, research programs, government organizations, social service agencies, religious organizations, cultural societies—in short, all nonprofit agencies—need to raise funds in order to continue their programs. *Development* is another name for fundraising.

If fundraising appeals to you, you can seek information from the Development department at any of the institutions listed above where substantial fundraising is conducted.

Fundraising projects are done in many different ways, from computerized letters to telephone campaigns. Colleges conduct very personal fundraising drives, using alumni who sometimes know each other. Social service agencies often solicit funds from banking and insurance institutions that are known for their philanthropy. For people who enjoy dealing with corporate officers and public relations representatives, fundraising can be an exciting occupation.

There are also many large companies that specialize in fundraising. They employ not only fundraisers but also account executives who service large accounts.

Another fundraising technique is the proposal, written by a *proposal writer*. The proposal is a structured document, written along suggested guidelines, that outlines a plan for executing a project using government or private funds. A college, for instance, might write a proposal requesting funds to recruit and educate thirty minority students. This same college probably writes many proposals in order to raise funds for other worthy causes.

If you like the orderly, structured writing that includes budgets and time frames for the completion of items, and if you like the challenge of writing a proposal worthy of funding, look into this field. Universities pay very well for this type of specialist.

Job Analyst. Job analysts in industry and government interview employees and supervisors in order to prepare job descriptions explaining the precise duties of the job and the accompanying responsibilities. From the information thus gathered, training and skill requirements are established for employees, and their wages are set.

Salaries in this field are excellent, about $20,000 to start. Employment can be found in most large companies, particularly banks, insurance companies, and large manufacturing companies, as well as in many parts of government.

Engineering Aide. This position is best suited to math and science majors. The aide helps an engineer run scientific experiments, calculate results, make drawings, and design models for experimental equipment. He or she may be involved in manufacturing, sales, and customer relations, too.

Qualifications for the position can be gained through work experience, on-the-job training, and some training in engineering or drafting.

Internship Developer. One of the hats I wore when I worked at a college was that of internship developer, a truly interesting role, which was instrumental in making my transition into business easier because through it I met managers who were helpful to me. The internships I developed were for former teachers and re-entry women.

What does an internship developer do?

I contacted local companies and social service agencies and asked for an internship that matched the interests of a particular student—from gerontology to technical writing. The intern then received on-the-job training working under an experienced supervisor. The advantages were twofold: the intern was able to try out a particular field before making a commitment of further education, and was able to form a network of people who were very helpful with his or her future career. In more than half the cases, the intern was asked to stay on as a paid employee.

Look to high schools, colleges, the government, and industry for these prized positions. If there is no program in your local area, propose one, and write yourself a job! Internship development permits you to deal directly with presidents and managers—an excellent way to broaden your own career education and to provide a high level of networking. (See the Bibliography for sources of internship programs in the United States.)

Legal Assistant/Paralegal. Since this is the fastest-growing field of all occupations, finding a job in it should be relatively easy, if you have the right credentials.

Educational requirements vary from state to state, so to check on those in your state you should make an appointment at a few legal firms, large and small, to make inquiries as to a correct course of action; companies may accept your present degree or may require paralegal courses or a paralegal certificate. Paralegals are used differently according to the specialty of the law firm—from wills to real estate work to research on briefs—so you have your own research to do in order to discover your own interests. This study will be helpful, because it will clarify your affinity for this type of work.

Teachers have taken the paralegal route and then decided to become lawyers when they found out that they loved the work.

Working as a legal assistant or as a paralegal could be the first step to becoming a lawyer.

Librarian. We are currently in the midst of an information explosion. It is the job of the librarian to link the public with all kinds of data, past and present.

A trip I took recently to the Library of Congress in our capital revealed that cataloguing jobs are open to people with a B.A. Teachers who have wanted to try out this field have been hired by libraries with the provision that they would take a master's degree in Library Science if they want to be promoted to Librarian.

There are two different types of library work: user services and technical services. The user services librarian works with the public, usually in a reference capacity or at the circulation desk. Technical services librarians are concerned with the processing of the library materials and do not deal with the public; they may be acquisition librarians and cataloguers. The information science specialist is another kind of technical services librarian; the specialist manages technical collections in government or research and must often be familiar with programming equipment and microfilm technology.

Library positions usually require a master's degree in library science. Jobs can be found in public libraries, hospitals, industry, banks, schools, museums, government, and research departments of all types of businesses.

This field is growing slowly but should pick up between 1985 and 1990. Salaries average $15,000; industry has the highest levels, from about $18,000 to $20,000 for entry-level positions.

Manager. I have included this general category so that teachers will realize their potentials as managers.

In the beginning of this chapter, I spoke of the entry-level position as the way to get a foot in the door of a company. But there are also companies that will hire candidates as managers and put them through an in-house training program. Seek out large companies and inquire into their procedures; utility companies and insurance companies are likely to be receptive, as are department store chains and specialty shops.

Another entree to managerial positions is the master's degree in business administration. The M.B.A. is one of the most desirable degrees in the job market today. Last year the students who graduated with this degree were snatched up by government agencies, business, and industry. The starting salaries of graduates from the best business schools, like Harvard and Wharton, were the highest paid to any graduates—up to $50,000.

Why is the M.B.A. considered to be such a valuable degree?

The continued growth in computer usage has provided institutions with tools that can simplify short- and long-term planning. The data that is retrieved from the computer needs to be analyzed; this can be done by the business school graduate, especially the one with strong skills in finance and marketing.

The M.B.A. program trains individuals who wish to enter management. Courses usually include marketing techniques, accounting, economics, advertising, business English, and personnel procedures. Women and minorities with business management degrees have at least as good a chance of finding employment as do men. (Be aware, however, that 55,000 graduates with M.B.A.s are now hitting the marketplace each year.)

Market Researcher. The year 1984 saw a rise in market research, probably because of the recession and increased competition in the marketplace.

The researcher uses reference books and trade journals in order to study the competition's products and advertising campaign literature; conducts feasibility studies; and performs other tasks related to the sale of products, ideas, or services—from the use of computer products to the popularity of a particular television show.

Market research is one of the fastest-growing industries. The increase regionally is as follows: 82 percent in the Southeast, 80 percent in the Midwest, 33 percent in the Southwest, and 21 percent in the Northeast.

Market research is one field in which teachers are especially qualified, because it involves marshaling facts and then drawing conclusions from them; a few basic courses in marketing and research techniques can easily be acquired.

Look for these positions in banks, brokerage companies, industry, and publishing companies; salaries vary from $18,000 to $20,000 for entry-level positions and $25,000 if you have an M.B.A.

Medical Assistant/Paramedic. In states where it is permitted, some physicians have trained their assistants to do a great deal of the work that does not require licensing as either a nurse or a doctor: interviewing patients in order to get their medical histories; running diagnostic blood and urine analyses; talking on the telephone to ascertain patients' complaints, relaying medical advice, or soothing an agitated or anxious patient. In addition, physicians' assistants may discuss dietary restrictions, outline exercise routines, and explain simple physical therapies. These same individuals may also perform any or all of the duties executed by the office manager.

These jobs are not readily available; however, they have been successfully sought out and won by assertive individuals. There are courses given in some states to train physicians' assistants. The salary is excellent, and the rewards of working in the field of medicine are psychologically satisfying.

Nontraditional Careers. If you have envied your father who is a bricklayer or your uncle who is a plumber, you don't have to be envious anymore.

For years women have been excluded from or advised against selecting careers traditionally held by men, but all that has changed. Women are now becoming plumbers, telephone company linesmen, drafters, technicians, policewomen, machine operators—or whatever. For the most part, holding these jobs is psychologically easier today, as far as harassment goes; many women have already paved the way. Because men have traditionally held these jobs, the salaries are comparatively high.

I mention nontraditional careers as possibilities, not because teachers have been drawn to nontraditional jobs in great numbers but to open this idea up to you as an option; there are teachers who have taken this route, and why not? Plumbers are usually entrepreneurs and can earn from $40,000 to $50,000 a year—nothing to take for granted, especially since plumbers are in demand; other jobs pay hourly wages that vary with the particular job sought. Most nontraditional jobs are union-scaled and union-controlled.

Office Manager. Office managers can be found wherever there are large numbers of people concentrated in one area, such as in law firms, publishing companies, accounting firms, hospitals, doctor's offices, government offices, banks, insurance companies, and industry.

The teacher possesses the potential to administer all managerial functions. Take, for example, the duties of an office manager in a group medical practice: working effectively with clientele; ordering all the medical supplies and equipment; billing patients; and arranging the doctors' schedules for office hours, operations, conferences, speeches, and dinner engagements. Doctors like to do doctoring; a good office manager is a blessing, and is usually paid accordingly, with salaries starting at $20,000.

Project Director or Manager. Social service and government agencies often receive funds or grants for a particular project. Most of these projects require the kind of management that a teacher could readily handle. The duties associated with these positions are to plan, direct, and coordinate the activities of a designated project and to set its aims, goals, and objectives. In addition, the director monitors the funds, confers with the staff to outline the plans, and later monitors staff progress. At the end of the project the director submits a final report.

Colleges and business schools also hire people to fill this position. Salaries are in the range of $20,000 to $25,000.

Purchasing Agent. Purchasing is a field I know very well because my brother works as a purchasing agent.

The remark isn't meant to be sexist, but female and male purchasing agents have both told me that purchasing is a natural for women because they are accustomed to shopping around for the best price—essentially the role of a purchasing agent.

There isn't a hospital, a college, or a business that doesn't need to purchase paper goods, office supplies, desks, copying machines, or industrial parts. In a small company the purchases are made by a secretary or an officer (my secretary and I both do the purchasing), but in medium-sized and large companies a purchasing agent does the buying. The nature of the work is such that as a purchasing agent you develop a list of vendors (people from whom you decide to buy), keeping in mind that you want to buy at the best price. It stands to reason that large companies buy enormous amounts of supplies and materials and often have large purchasing departments with people specializing in certain categories. Since these supplies may be needed for a surgical operation in a hospital, for example, you can see that keeping good control of inventory is also vital to any operation. (Another pun? Horrors.) The person who pushes the vendors to deliver the merchandise on a timely basis is the expediter, a lower-level position. A purchasing agent is on the managerial level.

Teachers have used the expediting and purchasing routes to break into a new field and have either stayed at it and risen to the top or have used it as a springboard into personnel. (Two former teachers have had huge success: one is presently earning $37,000 as a purchasing agent; the other has become a Human Resources Manager and is earning $45,000 at age 31—a former Spanish teacher who had set two-year goals for her career.)

Quality Assurance. If I were asked by a teacher (or anyone) to name the one field in industry in which I receive the most job orders and that had a high potential for growth both financially and professionally, I would answer: Quality Assurance.

The Japanese have made the United States extremely aware of its deficiencies in the realm of quality. Because of all the publicity and the subsequent recognition by American companies that the United States is losing its competitive edge in the marketplace, quality assurance has taken a front seat in industry. Dr. W. Edwards Deming has been in the forefront of this movement because of his introduction of statistical quality control.

The function of quality assurance departments in businesses from cosmetic companies to high-tech manufacturers is to oversee, inspect, and control the quality of any item that comes in or out of the facility. You may think that quality is a simple matter but it is not, because employees are often not committed to perfection and because some companies are more interested in shipments (because shipments determine profitability). If you decide to look into this field, find a company that *is* committed to quality; most companies are.

If you are more or less a perfectionist, have mathematical ability (in some cases, statistics and calibrations are necessary), and would like to get into this field, decide on your interests—cosmetics, computers, audio equipment, and so on—and speak to a manager in a quality assurance department. There are special quality institutes that have sprung up to train people, so you can find out who their client companies are. Salaries in this field start low but grow rapidly. Job-hopping is common in this field, and part-time is available (three months at a time). Ex-math teachers can earn $30,000 after three years and $45,000 within six or seven years, if they are good at what they do and can manage people well.

Which career seems to hold the most appeal to you? A career in banking? A career in the development department of a hospital? Or as a curriculum developer in industry? Whatever career you choose, with the proper techniques to conduct your job campaign your dream career can become a reality; Chapter 13 holds the key to the rainbow; it describes the techniques to transport you into your new field of endeavor.

11. How to Get A Job If You Really Want to Teach

I've been educated to be a teacher and I want to teach."
If you really want to teach and you have the patience, money, and time to devote to job-searching, it is possible to be successful. In addition, if you prepare ahead, persevere, and are even willing to relocate, your chances will improve immeasurably. Despite the layoffs, teachers do find jobs—but only those teachers who prepare active plans and strategies.

Adult education, continuing education, teacher training in-service centers, and individual communities conduct programs using trainers, facilitators, instructors, and so on—all terms for teachers. If you read your newspaper and educational journals carefully, you will discover new sources of employment: grants, programs, business schools, and so on. Completing a specialized college course or two could qualify you to teach English, basic mathematics, employment-seeking skills, or English as a second language. Teachers in these fields instruct youth, the uneducated, the unemployed, the disadvantaged, dropouts, and veterans, as well as business students and teachers who elect to upgrade their own professional skills.

Since your resume and cover letter are passports into the working world, be certain to have these ready as early as possible. Remember, since most schools start hiring in February, it is a good idea to send your resume around again at that time, even if you've already mailed it earlier. A letter or resume sent in November may be in the circular file by the time the administrators get around to hiring in February. Sometimes, too, schools are overwhelmed with registrants as late as August or September, so be sure to call at that time.

College Placement Offices. If you are a senior in college, your placement office can help you with most of your preparation. Seek out your counselor and find out about resume-writing workshops, recruiters from other schools, and placement services. An early start can put you out in front before the competition gets there.

Graduates, too, can call and visit nearby college placement offices. Services are generally free to alumni; a nominal fee may be charged to others. Inquire into the kinds of services they provide:

- Do they have job listings for teachers?
- Do they provide placement?
- Have they any friends you may use in networking?

Don't be a stranger in the placement office; if news of a job opening arrives on a day you are there, it could be yours!

Departments of Education. Almost all state departments of education have free listings of teaching openings that are available at any given time. Look in your telephone directory and become familiar with the office. Jobs turn up at odd times of the year, so keep the process going. State departments also hire teachers as program administrators. Have you considered that possibility?

Teacher's Associations. If you are willing to relocate, join the national association pertaining to your field of specialization; most association newsletters contain job openings. Your local librarian will show you where to find the reference book on United States associations. French teachers, for example, may contact:

American Association of Teachers of French
Placement Bureau
AATF National Headquarters
59 East Armory Avenue
Champaign, IL 61820

Private Teacher-Placement Agencies. You may want to (or have to) consider calling upon a private employment agency. At such an agency there is no charge for *information*. If the agency is reliable it should be able to advise you about the availability of positions in your specialty. If you decide to list with it, learn what its fee is, because if you find a job through its efforts, there will be a charge. Although such agencies prefer experienced candidates, they take inexperienced ones as well. Teachers are particulary needed in such fields as math, science (usually on the secondary level), vocational subjects, elementary counseling, foreign languages, and special education. Openings exist in urban areas and in locations where there is a concentration of Chicanos, blacks, Indians, Orientals, and Puerto Ricans.

One advantage of working with an agency is that it will often hear of emergency openings from principals who are anxious to fill a position quickly—but be sure you check newspaper and state listings before you go to an agency, unless it is free of cost to you.

One reputable agency lists the following as advice to college students:

- A good college grade point average can help even if you have no experience.
- Keep your geographical preference as wide as possible.
- Experience in the Peace Corps or Vista is very advantageous.

Sunday Newspaper Ads. Sunday is the best day to look for ads. Check your newspaper for a special section that contains teacher openings; most papers have one. If you find an opening advertised, call the school and make an appointment. Don't use the mail only; your chances will improve if you go in person.

Day Care Centers. "Learning to read is the most important part of a child's education," says a district manager of Kinder-Care, the largest day care corporation in the United States and Canada.

Started in 1969, Kinder-Care now operates more than 835 centers in 40 states and Canada and caters to the infant, the preschooler, and the child from six to twelve years old, in an afterschool program. In 1981 Kinder-Care also established day-care centers, in cooperation with industry, to serve the working parent; a center is set up right at the company or nearby. For the teacher who works in industry day-care, there is a double advantage, professionally speaking: employment for oneself as well as the opportunity to form a huge network, should the teacher decide to work in industry one day.

Although starting salaries are low—from $10,400 to $13,000—the company does promote from within. One teacher who started as a substitute has become the company's training manager; others have become district and regional directors.

There is another advantage to working at Kinder-Care. If you have children of your own, you will receive a fifty percent discount if they attend the center, although infants are not included in this plan. The company provides such benefits as paid holidays and sick leave for teachers who work more than twenty hours a week.

To inquire about this day-care giant (it is on the stock exchange), contact the Public Relations Director, Kinder-Care, Inc., Executive Park Drive, Box 2151, Montgomery, AL 36197; telephone (205) 277–5090.

Write an Article. While you are job-hunting, spend some time in your local school library looking through teachers' magazines and publications. If an idea for an article occurs to you, try to place it with a professional magazine, your local newspaper, or one of the professional teachers' organizations. A published article carries with it a measure of prestige, establishes you as a writer, and is a good job-hunting tool; it may even help you discover hidden talents that could lead to an alternative career.

Apply for a Grant. Many people write grant proposals in order to receive funding for projects. One teacher received a grant to start a local newspaper that continued successfully after that money ran out. There are 30,000 private foundations that distribute a total of $26 billion each year.

Take a few hours and look over the books on grants that you will find in your library; perhaps some creative idea, related to teaching, will leap to mind and motivate you to seek a grant. Two such books are *The Foundation Directory*, Ninth Edition, (New York: Foundation Center, 1983), and *The Individual's Guide to Grants*, Judith B. Margolin (New York: Plenum Publishing, 1983).

Volunteer or Create a Job. As you seek a job and gather information on possibilities, you may discover an environment that really appeals to you. It could be beneficial to volunteer your services, especially if your resume would be improved by the addition of experience in that particular field. Very often, volunteer positions turn into jobs.

You may also find that your community lacks a certain facility: for example, a youth center. Many people have seen a particular need and sold the idea to the proper authorities. Think about it, and keep your eyes open—a little ingenuity goes a long way.

Visits to Schools. Take out a map of your area and draw a circle with as wide a radius as you can consider. Locate all the schools in that area. If you ask, the school administrative office in each district or town will send you a map or listing of all the schools under its jurisdiction. Try a bold approach: appear on the scene, resume in hand. Sending letters and resumes in the mail is okay, but you are much more than words on paper. You are many-faceted, palpable, and more convincing than any resume can be. If you are in luck, a teacher will have moved out of town suddenly. Give it a try—and good luck!

Start a Letter Campaign. If you cannot reach a wide geographical area in person, it is perfectly acceptable to send letters and resumes to as many principals as possible. But don't be too disappointed if you never hear from the school. Why? Because principals receive many letters and do not always have the time, help, or postage to respond to each one—a sign of the times. Anyway, you only need to hear from *one* principal. Right?

Teacher's Aide; Tutor; Substitute. If nothing else works and you have knocked on all the doors you can, consider becoming a

Sample Letter for Recent Graduates

4127 Gable Avenue
West Palm Beach, Florida 33409
(305) 555-1717

February 7, 1985

Ms. Jane L. Halsy, Principal
Harris School
West Palm Beach, Florida 33409

Dear Ms. Halsy:

At your suggestion I am forwarding my resume to you in order to be considered for a teaching position in the third grade.

During my senior year at Wheelock College, I worked with a group of non-English-speaking minority students, and implemented a special dance program in which they learned to speak English through the medium of dance. The program was written up in the local newspaper; a copy of the article is enclosed.

My ability to speak Spanish would be very helpful to the students attending your school.

You may contact me at home during the next week. Because I am eager for an interview, I will keep in touch with you.

Sincerely,

Wendy Morgan

Wendy Morgan

teacher's aide, tutor, or substitute. If you become recognized as dependable, professional, and available, you could become indispensable. When I was substituting as a French teacher, I was asked to take a regular position once or twice a year, simply because I was around. The administration knew me, knew my dependability, and turned to me when an opening occurred. In educational as in business circles, visibility counts. Substituting in several schools during the year increases your noticeability and chances of employment. Mid-semester openings sometimes occur, and you may be there to fill the spot.

A town or city administrative office will be able to provide population statistics, so ask for them. It makes sense to select a younger community with a growing population, if you can. Otherwise, you might land a job only to be "excessed" the following year and forced to repeat the job-hunting process. If you have no other choice, then you may want to take your chances.

Teaching Abroad: Four Thousand Openings. Would you believe that every year there are approximately four thousand teaching, library, counseling and administrative openings in American and International English-speaking schools overseas?

In addition to the large number of schools operated by the United States Department of Defense for children of armed forces members stationed abroad, there are approximately four thousand openings in private, independent, community schools serving the children of overseas Americans, local citizens who want their children to have an American education, and the children of the third-world countries.

A hundred and forty-seven foreign countries seek native English-speaking teachers for their schools, universities, and language instruction centers.

There are so many overseas schools and opportunities that it is a tremendous task to find out where the openings are at any one time.

Your public library can direct you to number of reference books on the subject, but the best overall current information about school openings around the world can be obtained from a service that specializes in this field. It is called Education Information Service, P.O. Box 662X, Newton Lower Falls, MA 02162.

Teachers of English and all other school subjects as well as teachers of English as a second language are in great demand in exotic countries. I have a cousin who has been teaching in Hawaii for several years; she doesn't ever want to return stateside.

So if you want to teach à l'étranger, there are openings available. But be aware: you may never want to return, either!

12. Looking to 1990: The Best Careers

If Helen of Troy launched a thousand ships in her day, the period 1985 to 1990 will launch thousands of teachers into new careers.

Which careers will they be?

Although teachers will find more opportunities open again in school systems (see the Introduction), interest in the more lucrative, competitive world of business and industry will continue to be present. The computer industry will provide the greatest growth and opportunity for advancement. Government statistics reveal other fields of growth, too, that you should know about.

In competition with high technology and the computer industry will be the health field, which will grow rapidly as we approach the end of this century.

What is the reason for this growth?

In the first place, the elderly are living longer, thus creating needs that include nutrition, transportation, recreation, nursing, medical treatment, clinics, and research-oriented programs. In the second place, people born in the post–World War II baby

Job Title	Percent of Increase in the 80s
Paralegal personnel	108.9%
Computer operators	71.6
Computer systems analysts	67.8
Office machine servicers	59.8
Physical therapists	50.9
Computer programmers	48.9
Employment interviewers	47.0
Speech and hearing personnel	46.6
Travel agents	43.4
Nurses	39.6
Accountants	26.5
Service industries	24.0
Elementary school teachers	19.5

also:

Psychologists
Electrical engineers
Dieticians
Economists
Architects
Veterinarians

boom are now between 35 and 40 years old and have vast medically-related needs. Third, greater public awareness and subsequent government legislation to serve the handicapped has caused a proliferation of programs and services. In the fourth place, the infant mortality rate has been lowered and more babies are surviving; however, they too may need special care.

In the above table you will see that the need for nurses and therapists is projected to grow between 39 and 50 percent. Former teachers who have made the decision to stay in the helping professions have made satisfying careers for themselves in these fields. For those who are interested, part-time jobs are available, and therapists' positions lend themselves to private practice. Another alternative, if you like a quasi-medical environment, is a medical employment agency, which provides medical establishments with nurses and other staff. Agencies are, however, part of the business sector.

Since therapists are in such demand, a description of the work they do is included.

Physical and Occupational Therapists. Therapists use special methods to relieve patients' pain or help patients adjust to temporary or permanent handicaps. Physical and occupational therapists must be creative because they design exercises or activities specifically to suit each patient's needs. Usually, the physical therapists create physically beneficial exercises and the occupational therapists design programs consisting of arts and crafts along with vocational and homemaking skills.

Children as well as adults are served in these programs, so therapists can often select their fields of interest. Our current enthusiasm for physical fitness and sports has raised the number of people who need the assistance of therapists, too.

In order to train as a therapist, you will need courses in the biological and physical sciences. Once you become both trained and experienced as a therapist you could find another source of employment as a teacher, because experienced personnel have found jobs in universities and hospitals and as administrators of clinics in industry.

Salaries start at about $18,000, but supervisors can earn $30,000. If the entrepreneurial spirit moves you, as it has with 14 percent of therapists, you can open your very own private practice.

Speech and Hearing Specialist. This is one field in which job opportunities will continue to be abundant over the next several years. About one out of every ten Americans has trouble with either speech or hearing. Specialists diagnose and provide the necessary treatment for these people. Some specialists teach in hospitals or universities, or are directors of clinics. Others are employed in their own practices and in public schools, colleges, clinics, research centers, and government agencies. In most states a graduate degree is a requirement. If part-time work is your goal, it is possible to attain it as a speech and hearing therapist.

Private companies, too, have entered this field; they coach executives and public figures who want to improve their images.

One fact is certain: hospitals, schools, and industrial clinics will open up their arms to you because the shortage of therapists is already endemic in all fifty states.

Social Worker. Recent legislation regarding the Social Security Act, national health insurance, and the expansion of existing programs in the fields of consumerism, rape, child abuse, drug and alcohol abuse, battered people, and aging is expected to open up many new jobs for social workers. Because there are so many graduates in this field, the competition will be keen.

If you have a B.A. you may be able to apply for a position as a case or group worker, but the possibility for advancement will be limited. A master's degree (M.S.W.) will open the door to jobs in administration, research, planning, and teaching.

In many ways social work is akin to teaching, because most of the work is done on a one-to-one basis. Social workers try to improve the condition and well-being of deprived, sick, and troubled people. They work in the community, in hospitals, in nursing homes, and for government agencies. They help people understand themselves better, they conduct activities for all age groups, and they arrange services for the elderly. For beginners in this field, the salaries are low, but teachers and administrators are paid quite well. As in teaching, the rewards can be high.

Gerontology. The field of gerontology—dealing with the elderly— is growing by leaps and bounds as the government becomes more responsive to the needs of all people, especially the elderly.

Colleges are opening up gerontology departments offering courses on all the issues that deal with the elderly; for example, consumerism, recreation, housing, health, nutrition, finance, education, employment, and transportation.

Throughout the country there are employment opportunities in councils on aging, home care agencies, nursing homes, hospitals, industry, and even local branches of teachers' associations where pre-retirement programs are run. Teachers can transfer their skills to this field with a modicum of new training; the experienced may find teaching opportunities, too.

13. Making It Happen

This chapter describes the entire process of career search and job change, from gathering data about career interests through considering the personal factors involved in a change to writing resumes and negotiating salary. The process is often trying, but it is nevertheless exciting because it involves self-discovery and personal growth.

While you are following through on the steps outlined in this chapter, you should also follow several other paths simultaneously, such as:

- Reading a few books on careers; there are lots of paperbacks available. (See Bibliography.)
- Taking a vocational test.
- Making a private appointment with a career counselor. Most colleges and universities provide this service for a nominal fee.
- Starting to interview a few friends, neighbors, or relatives in other fields. Conduct these interviews at their employ-

103

ment sites, and stick to business talk. Do not be afraid to ask for the names of other people in other fields. Widening your career knowledge is absolutely mandatory at this stage; almost all of us have mistaken ideas about other people's roles. There is always more to any job than our minds originally envisage.

The First Step: Organize Your Data

A good way to begin the process of self-discovery is by purchasing and filling a few manila folders, organizing them as follows:

Folder A: Interests. Place in here everything that seems to interest you as you read newspapers and magazines: a feature article on an art business; a story about someone doing a job that appeals to you; ads from Sunday's employment section of the newspaper. Don't discriminate at this point, but do some weeding later on. Remember, the key here is to select only those jobs that appeal to you.

Folder B: Network. Put index cards in this folder. On each card, place the name of someone you know. Continue this process until you have listed all your contacts—relatives, doctors, lawyers, neighbors, college professors. Also keep on the lookout for people in authoritative positions in fields that interest you—a personnel vice president whose name appeared in the newspaper, for instance. The purpose of these names is to provide you with a list of people you may interview for career information. Interviewing can provide a valuable show-and-tell occasion for your talents. By making a contact here and a contact there, you can also begin to establish your personal network of people who can be helpful in your job-hunting.

Folder C: Portfolio. You may want to start collecting data that pertains to past accomplishments. This could include certificates of commendation, special awards, evaluations, letters of recommendation, a resume, stories you have written, art work—anything that can build a constructive case for your qualifications for the jobs that you will be seeking. You will take this portfolio with you on interviews to document your successes and your work history.

The Second Step: Identify Skills

The next move is to identify your own skills, a step that teachers have sometimes found difficult. Go through the following list of skills quickly and locate your strengths by placing a plus mark (+) next to those you possess:

- Creative skills (be specific)
- Foreign language ability
- Sports ability
- Verbal skills
- Written skills
- Mathematical ability
- Ability to organize and coordinate
- Art and music abilities
- Leadership qualities
- Curriculum design experience
- (Other)

Now you can go back to this list and ponder your other skills; asking people who know you well to help you find your strengths has been valuable for those teachers who recognize their pupils' skills but who have trouble evaluating their own. If you are one of these people, taking an aptitude test is advisable; these are given at placement and counseling centers in colleges. Don't make the mistake of going to one of the high-powered counseling companies unless you have several thousand dollars to spend; it is just not worth the money, in my estimation.

The Third Step: Identify Job Titles

After you have made a list of the skills you possess, the next step is to identify job titles that embody these skills. The following lists will begin to lead you towards the translation of your own unique set of skills and interests into possible careers; other alternatives can be found throughout this book. Circle any job title that appeals to you or about which you would like to learn more. This is not meant to be a definitive list; it is a technique to get you thinking about careers you can pursue.

Jobs that use creative skills. Photographer; educational materials developer; curriculum developer; advertising account executive; public relations specialist; commissioner; instructor; entrepreneur; landscape designer; project director; conference coordinator; editor; interior designer; graphics illustrator; artist; recreation director; craft producer; writer for an in-house newsletter; author; copywriter; technical writer.

Jobs that use foreign language ability. College counselor; foreign student advisor; consul, or language center administrator; teacher of English as a second language in industry; translator (business or industry); textbook editor; Peace Corps administrator; Berlitz instructor.

Jobs that use sports ability. Instructor at a Y or a health club; sports announcer; college teacher; journalist; retail sports store manager.

Jobs that use strong verbal skills. Fundraiser; purchaser; employment interviewer; radio or televison announcer; counselor, social worker; trainer; personnel worker; public relations specialist; collection agent; administrative assistant; advertising account executive; affirmative action officer; commissioner; dean; coordinator; travel agent; real estate broker; salesperson; customer relations worker; director of alumni relations; admissions counselor; foreign student advisor; interior decorator; office manager; internship developer; job developer; legal assistant; manager; recreation director; systems analyst; adult education teacher; bank employee; lawyer; travel agent; stockbroker.

Jobs that use strong writing skills. Administrative assistant; admissions representative; advertising account executive; project director; research assistant; copywriter; public relations specialist; curriculum developer; educational materials developer; publishing house employee; writer for an in-house newsletter; legal assistant; legislative assistant; librarian; manager; customer relations supervisor; textbook editor; author; proposal writer; systems analyst; programmer; technical writer.

Jobs that use mathematics ability. Computer programmer; systems analyst; actuary; accountant; tax expert; lawyer; technical instructor; technical writer; financial aid director; fundraiser; administrator; affirmative action officer; proposal writer; consultant; bank employee; market researcher; corporate liaison specialist; curriculum developer; engineering aide; office manager; purchaser; quality and material control manager; personnel worker; urban planner.

Jobs that use the abilities to organize and coordinate. Project director; travel agent; conference coordinator; college dean; office manager; personnel manager; director of transportation or nutrition; supervisor of training; urban planner; landscape designer; entrepreneur; purchasing agent; fund raiser.

Brainstorming: Examples in Art and Music. Finding a job that suits you is often simply a matter of opening your eyes and considering every possible job related to your interest, no matter how far-fetched it may seem at first. If, for example, you are an art major or music teacher, you should consider:

- Choral group work
- Conducting
- Public relations in the music field
- Working for a record company
- Opening your own business
- Managing in a music association
- Making animated musical films
- Handling music therapy in hospitals and clinics
- Being a booking agent for musicians
- Being an administrator for an arts foundation
- Being a church choir director, organist, soloist, or choir member
- Being an accompanist in musical theater
- Administrating, producing, or directing a symphony orchestra, opera company, or music theater

There is not enough room here to list such possibilities for every field of interest, but these examples should give you an idea of how to brainstorm the many career options that are open to you.

Now, you are probably asking yourself, "How can I ever begin to find out all I need to know about these job titles?" Some of these titles are found under generic career titles. All of the following titles, for instance, fall under the general category of personnel: employment interviewer, recruiter, human resource specialist, trainer, and benefits administrator, so you would look under *Personnel* in career books. The bible for career information is a book called *The Occupational Outlook Handbook*. It is available in the reference section of all career centers and libraries. The handbook describes jobs in detail and tells you the type of educational background needed for them, the personal qualities sought, salaries, and the availability of jobs in a specific field. It is a book highly recommended for those seeking career information either for themselves or for members of the family.

The Fourth Step: Interviewing Professionals

After you have selected a few titles that appeal to you and that utilize some of your skills, you can start to interview people in your chosen fields; professionals are usually very receptive to inquiries. This kind of information-gathering may be the best way to sell *yourself* on a career, too. It it also a good way to dispel fantasies about what you expected the job to be like as opposed to what it really is like. Interviewing should be done in two stages, one very early in the data-gathering stage and again when you zero in on a career. In this manner you will learn more about the world outside the classroom.

If you don't know anyone in your field of interest, obtain a list of alumni from your college and call a few people. This really works! Alumni love to help other alumni.

Today's job-hunting calls for personal action. Try this: call a small agency or company; receptionists are generally friendly. Say that you are seeking information about a particular occupation, and ask who might be receptive to answering questions on XYZ occupation. You will be surprised at the results you will get.

Make an appointment or two. Look up the company first, in a business directory in the library, just to have a few impressive facts ready. Have a few questions ready to ask about the actual day-to-day responsibilities of the job and ask about cons of the job as well as the pros—in other words, the good and the bad aspects, if any.

Everyone loves this kind of interview; you will gain information, and the other person will be given a chance to relax and reminisce about the early days of her or his career. One day the person you are talking to just might hire you, or may help by giving you names of other people in the profession. It's okay to ask for names, addresses, and telephone numbers; this is how your network can begin to work for you. Never be afraid to obtain all the information you need. Are you being an opportunist? No, you are creating your own opportunity. When you have made it, you will, in turn, help others.

The Fifth Step: Narrow It Down

When you have gathered sufficient information about the careers in which you are interested, the time for hard decision-making will be at hand. Without a specific career decision, you cannot begin a plan of action.

You must be ready to answer these questions!

- What do I really want to do? (Narrow your list to two or three career choices.)
- Have I decided that I need specific credentials? If not, what plans must I make to gather more information?
- In what environment am I most comfortable? Social service? Business? Education? Government?
- Is the size of the institution important to me?
- In what geographical areas am I willing to work? (The wider the better.)
- What are my priorities? Money? Prestige? Any job at any cost? Security? Travel? A helping profession? Volunteerism? Part-time? Full-time?

The Sixth Step: The Resume

There are several reasons to go through the process of writing a resume. Preparing your resume helps you focus on careers that interest you. In professional circles, moreover, it is expected that you produce a resume; it is an aid in selling yourself to a prospective buyer. Don't flinch at the word *selling*—that's a fact. The resume often arrives on someone's desk before you arrive. If the appearance is attractive and if you have presented your credentials appealingly, it will be a successful sales instrument, as a jacket is on a new book.

The *real* purpose of the resume is to obtain an interview: *no interview, no job*. Although you will depend on your network as the best method of getting an interview, sometimes you will answer an ad or send a resume along to someone who may have influence.

There are different types of resumes. Look over the types and select the style that suits you best. If you are pursuing very diverse fields, *write a different resume for each one.*

General Rules for Preparing a Resume

1. Do not mention handicaps or divorce.

2. Do not list height or weight unless it is relevant to the job.

3. Do not write a chronological resume; if you don't want to teach, write a functional resume, listing accomplishments.

4. Do not mention dates if you think it could hurt your cause.

5. Do not write your reason for leaving a job; explain at the interview.

6. Do not list the names of references. You'll want to call them to see if they are still located where you think they are.

7. Do state salary requirements, but be certain you know the going rates.

8. Do not attempt to list every single thing you have ever done. Keep facts relevant to your objective.

9. Do not name religious or political affiliations *unless* they are job-related. Why test prejudices?

10. Do put your education first, if it reads well, or place it on the bottom if it doesn't. Do include special awards, honors, and so on.

11. Do write a job objective. If you don't know what you want, who will? Personnel people do not have the time to play guessing games. But keep it brief.

12. Do write a first draft. Reread, after a few days, and rewrite if necessary.

13. Do have someone check your spelling and question the contents. *Everyone* makes mistakes, but you must try to eliminate them.

14. Do use an excellent typewriter with a carbon film ribbon, or hire a professional typist. It is not necessary to have the resume printed.

15. Do try to keep your resume to one page, leaving good margins at the top and sides and between sections. Easy reading is important.

16. Do use pale, colored paper. (One manager told me he once selected a pale blue resume from a thick stack of white ones.)

17. Do use standard-size paper, 8½ by 11 inches.

18. Do examine your resume. Does it (1) state your job objective? (2) list the accomplishments that follow the objective? (3) make a clear statement to the reader?

A first letter to a prospective employer will not usually bring a response. When you mail only one letter, the possibility of your being disappointed is magnified, because the human tendency is to expect immediate success. Don't fall into that trap. Mail out five or six resumes and letters at a time. Every hundred resumes mailed brings a response of only from two to five requests for interviews. That is why using or creating a large network is so much better in obtaining interviews.

The Seventh Step: Active Looking

Now that you have chosen your field, how do you start your job hunt?

Part of any job campaign is activity and making yourself known. If you are working, you will have to use your after-work hours, although you could use some of your vacation time. But the rule is to be active and visible. If you stay home and wait for the telephone to ring, you will be invisible. Invest in an answering machine, and be seen by people who are in a position to help, hire, or refer you. The following steps summarize much of the job-hunting advice of this book:

1. Join a professional organization in the field you want to enter; ask questions and make friends.

2. Visit college placement offices.

3. Seek out friends in business.

4. Are there any computerized job banks in your area? Visit them. State employment offices often have computerized systems.

5. Place an ad in trade or association newspapers (they're free). Your reference librarian can be exceptionally helpful in obtaining sources and addresses.

6. Keep your eyes open to new projects as you read the newspaper. Think creatively and act upon your ideas.

7. Attend affirmative action career seminars and job fairs.

8. Visit private employment agencies and be convincing—they will send good prospects on interviews, or call a company or two for them.

9. Join an association in your field of interest. Sign up for a committee; continue to broaden your network.

10. Women's organizations often serve as links to employers seeking women. Join!

11. Use your Christmas card list to discover new sources of employment and to maintain your network. Don't think that asking for help from the family shows lack of independence—that's nonsense. We all need all the help we can get.

12. Read the obituaries. The sad fact is that people die and create job openings.

13. Obtain and use a list of local alumni from your alma mater. If you went to school in Lower Slobbovia and now live in Los Angeles, you can bet your last dollar that other alumni have moved to Los Angeles, too. (Would anyone actually stay in Lower Slobbovia?)

14. Speak to your political representatives. They know many influential people.

15. The local Chamber of Commerce keeps tabs on new companies. Ask there for a directory of members and the names of a few people who may be in a position to help you. Drop in, introduce yourself, and make them an offer they won't be able to refuse.

The Process of Change

Time and patience. The average job takes six months to obtain. Although a thorough familiarization with the job-seeking process can hasten this timetable, it is doubtful that this period can be significantly shortened unless a friend or someone from your network drops a job into your lap. So remember, everyone else in your position is sweating it out, too. Pat yourself on the back to keep yourself going. (Did you ever see Jimmy Connors on the tennis court? He pumps himself up to keep psyched up. Learn from a pro.)

Management by objectives. Many businesses operate under a system called Management by Objectives. Setting objectives for yourself in your career helps you clarify your thoughts and crystalize your plans. Use a large calendar to set dates and time-tables for what you have decided would be reasonable goals to accomplish. Ease up on the schedule when you must, however, to avoid the feeling that you are living inside a pressure cooker.

Commitment and focus. These two factors must be strongly stressed. If your goal is an alternative career, it is necessary to commit yourself to that goal and make it your number-one priority. Successful people agree that one major project is all that should be undertaken if success is to be achieved. This does not mean that obligations and leisure activities are to be abandoned; it means only that you may have to set limits and postpone a few pleasures until a later date.

Focus your energies in the direction in which you have decided to go, after having conferred with family, friends, and several professionals who are knowledgeable about the job market.

Select the career path for which *you* feel best suited and don't stray off your course: a frog that jumps from bank to bank may end up in the water.

Risk. Whether you are employed or unemployed, seeking a career in a different field means accepting risk. Risk comes with change and involves insecurity, fear of the unknown, the possibility of harder work, a lowered income, the need for more education or training, the challenge of meeting new people, the testing of ability, the threat of possible failure, the acceptance of a geographical change, the loss of friends, and possibly even too much success. Examine it and weigh it, then accept it or reject it—you're the one who must decide. Of course, a new career may also bring a heightened existence and a strong sense of accomplishment, as it has for thousands of teachers.

The Pre-Interview Checklist

1. Do research on the company if you have time, or call the public relations department to obtain information on: volume of business per annum (this year and last year, so that you can determine the trend); type of business or agency; and number of

Sample Resume of Ex-Teacher

This resume describes a teacher who collected milk money and money for field trips, ran the school newspaper, submitted departmental reports, and so on.

SUZANNE HILL
314 Beacon Street
Waltham, Massachusetts 02154
(617) 555-3127

OBJECTIVE: A position in Public Relations with opportunity to demonstrate creativity, interpersonal skills, layout/design capability; and computer knowledge.

EDUCATION: Northeastern University, B.A., 1974
Major: English

Boston University, 1977
Courses: Media Design, Writing for the Media; Advertising; BASIC I, II; COBOL; Technical writing.
Computers: IBM, NEC, Wang, Apple.

EXPERIENCE:

Public Relations: Conceived, designed, edited, printed newspaper.
Compared costs, formats, concepts with other editors.
Reduced costs of printing.
Located new source of advertising.
Maintained contact with media personnel to publicize activities.

Administrative: Solicited, received funds.
Submitted plans, budgets, reports.
Improved scheduling of meetings.
Innovated timesaving devices.
Reduced costs of purchases.

Interpersonal: Introduced highly-successful counseling technique.
Elected to chair special committee.
Instituted a successful group recreation plan.
Selected as liaison between agencies.

Professional Societies: Newspaper Guild
Northeastern University Alumni Association

Sample Resume for Recent Graduate

ROBERT NELSON
2612 Bowman Lane   Chicago, Illinois 60680
(312) 555-9402

Objective: To work hard in a teaching position at inspiring young minds with the joy of learning.

Education: B.A., University of Chicago, 1984
Major: Elementary education
Minor: Humanities—dance, drama
Best Subjects: English; mathematics; child psychology, modern dance; computer applications; (Apple, TRS–80)

Work Experience:
1977, 1976   COUNSELOR
Assisted three teachers in camp program for retarded students.
Created an original play.
Taught mathematics by incorporating subject matter into original material.
Choreographed and presented play for parents.

The funds received from this work experience contributed toward college educational expenses.

School Activities:

1975–1978   POLITICAL CAMPAIGNER on campus and in town offices of two candidates.
DANCE CLUB member and former club president.
STUDENT ADVISER to incoming freshman.

These activities provided a realistic training ground in the development of personal, social, and intellectual skills.

REFERENCES AVAILABLE IN PLACEMENT OFFICE

Sample of a Functional Resume

To this resume you may add a **Work History** section, if you wish, listing names of companies, schools, etc.

JANICE WARNER
12 Pleasant Street   Westport, Connecticut 06880
(203) 555-1526 (home)
(203) 555-4688 (business)

Objective

To join a creative team in a **Training Department** in business or industry.

Education

M.A., University of Maryland
B.A., Stanford University

Workshops: Career Development; Organizational Behavior; Needs Assessment; Computer Usage; BASIC I, II, (DEC; IBM PC)

Experience

COORDINATOR
of research project involving business and governmental agencies throughout Westport, Greenwich, and Darien.
TEACHER-TRAINER
in Adult Education departments of two colleges: Organizational Behavior; Career Development; Value Clarification.

CURRICULUM DEVELOPMENT
Developed models for Value Clarification and Career Development.

TEACHER
in elementary school; innovated a reporting system that resulted in a special commendation.

Affiliations

American Society for Training and Development
National Society of Educators
Association for Supervision and Curriculum Development
League of Women Voters
Political Party

References Upon Request

Sample Cover Letter

357 Heron Avenue
Atlantic City, New Jersey 08400
(609) 555-9941

August 2, 1985

Dr. Warren Knapp, Director
Joseph A. Laszo Center
64 North Carolina Avenue
Atlantic City, New Jersey 08401

Dear Dr. Knapp,

I am enclosing my resume for the position of Curriculum Developer,
as advertised in the New York Times on August 1.

Having previously completed the development of an ESL curriculum
that was successfully used throughout the city of Philadelphia,
I believe that I could adapt this curriculum to your area with
equally favorable results.

My familiarity with funding sources should be helpful, also, in
seeking future revenue for your projects.

The Laszo Center's reputation for excellence has prompted my desire
to seek a position with you.

Because I cannot be reached conveniently during the day, I will call
your office on Thursday with the hope of setting up an appointment.

Sincerely,

Jill Kutchin

Jill Kutchin

employees this year compared with those last year. Minimal information is better than none.

2. Dress conservatively and appropriately. Institutions have different dress codes. It is suggested that women avoid wearing pants to the interview, although pants are perfectly acceptable once you are hired.

3. Rehearse the questions and answers in the following section.

4. Have your portfolio ready with samples of your work, extra resumes, lists of accomplishments, letters of commendation, and any questions you may want to ask.

5. Be sure you have clear, accurate directions to the meeting place, and know its address and telephone number.

6. Do you know the interviewer's full name and title?

7. Do you know the title of the job you are applying for?

8. When you arrive at your destination (early, of course), sit in the lobby and relax. Take a deep breath and then breathe normally.

9. Smile—it helps to relax your entire body.

Following are some general common-sense rules. Adapt them to suit yourself.

The Interview "Don'ts"

Don't wear a coat into the office; hold it on your arm.

Don't shake hands unless a hand is offered. (Some people don't like to touch strangers.) If you do shake hands, grasp firmly.

Don't put your papers on the desk (private property).

Don't begin with a negative remark. (My, this room is stuffy!)

Don't smoke; you may however, accept *one* cigarette, if offered (if you smoke!).

Don't speak indistinctly.

Don't try to ingratiate yourself by betraying confidences.

Don't apologize for your age.

Don't keep stressing your need for a job; stress your skills.

Don't say you can do everything; instead, define your fields of knowledge.

Don't display a feeling of inferiority.

Don't apologize for lack of business experience. Be confident that your skills are applicable.

Don't lie. If you don't know, say so. But state your ability to learn.

Don't appear to be listening to the conversation if the phone rings.

Don't be cynical.

Don't hesitate to fill out applications. (A negative response could irritate the interviewer. Be aware of this risk.)

Don't hang around, prolonging the interview, when it should be over.

The Interview "Do's"

Do seek a job that will tax you almost to the peak of your potential. Don't take on much more or settle for much less. (If you have been searching for a long time and need the money, you can take a lower-level job and use it as a steppingstone.)

Do make an appointment early in the day, before everyone is tired.

Do expect to be kept waiting in the lobby. (Don't crowd too much into your day. Allow from two to three hours for the interview, even if you don't need it.)

Do approach the employer with respectful dignity.

Do be polite and pleasant—smile. Proceed slowly, taking cues from the interviewer, but don't be cute.

Do remember that older employees, too, are capable, dependable, trainable, creative, experienced, promotable, energetic, enthusiastic, and so on.

Do let the interviewer feel in command.

Do assume an air of confidence.

Do look the interviewer in the eye, but don't stare him or her down.

Do be a good listener. You can gather useful information.

Do try to get an explanation of the responsibilities of the position and the criteria for employment. Use this to frame your answers.

Do recount experience you have had that would fit you for the job. Stress accomplishments.

Do recognize your limitations, but know your strengths, too.

Do ask questions for information or clarification.

Do *take the initiative* if the conversation lags or isn't going where you want.

Do establish a positive image.

Do answer questions honestly.

Do stress the *contribution* you can make: that's what you are there for.

Do use the employer's name during the interview.

Do indicate your flexibility and readiness to learn.

Do end the interview on a friendly note. Ask for a company brochure.

Do *ask* for the job, if you want it!

The Interview

There is no passport to a successful interview, but knowing what to expect can be very helpful. The interview is the key to the job offer, so understand the value of being prepared and of being convincing; if you are not convinced that you are an asset, then how can you convince anyone else?

Although teachers often express fear about having an interview, of all professionals they should feel the most confident. Isn't the sharing of information old hat to a teacher? An interview is a sharing, a give-and-take, an exchange, but be aware: it is definitely not a confessional—so never tell all.

As in all walks of life, in interviewing there are seasoned performers as well as bit players, so don't expect that the interviewer will necessarily have good interviewing skills. Many people in personnel started with the company straight out of high school and have been promoted; others will have a teaching degree (yes!) or a master's in industrial relations. Which person will be the best interviewer? Take your pick—it's impossible to predict. You may have to help the interviewer by leading into your qualifications and by asking questions. You do get better at interviewing, so don't go to your treasured place of employment first; wait until you can review your interviewing style.

What kind of atmosphere does the interviewer expect? Understanding the other person's point of view and the interpersonal dynamics from the other side of the table is good ammunition to have. The interviewer's state of mind is apt to be something like this:

"My day is long and busy. Sometimes there is a lot of tension caused by deadlines, reports, telephone calls, and interviewing. The last thing that I want to find opposite me is an adversary or a debater.

"I'm better than average at my job. So don't indicate, by word or by body action, that you could conduct a better interview, express yourself better, or take over my job. But speak up, don't be timid. Convince me that you want this job and would be a credit to the company. I really need to fill this position, so I hope that you're good!

"I'm an employment specialist and not a counselor; *you* should know what you want, what your five-year career goal is. I'll decide whether we can satisfy that goal. Don't say that you don't know what you want or that you want my job; both answers turn me off. Make up your mind *before* you job-hunt—and my job is *my* job.

"I'm a good listener. But don't make me uncomfortable with political speeches. We shouldn't use this time for debate (unless I'm interviewing you for a legislative position).

"I will respect your rights and you will respect mine. (If I make a mistake, it would help you to stay calm and be tactful.)

"I hope you fit our needs, but if not, let's part friends; you never know, I may call you at a later date."

One of the most intriguing suggestions I have ever heard is to play Japanese Tea Ceremony while the interview is being conducted. The ceremony is a polite, traditional, ritualistic affair. If the host sits "just so," the guest sits "just so." The host picks up his teacup "just so." The guest picks up his teacup "just so." And so on through the ritual. In other words, take your cues from the interviewer. Psychological studies of organizational behavior conclude that interviewers and employers hire people like themselves (although I have known many people to hire those they would *like* to be as well as those who will not outshine them). This does not suggest that you should make yourself over—presenting the real you is important—but personal chemistry does influence the buyer of your talents. Behavioral skill lies in *modifying* your behavior to specific situations.

If you should find that the interviewer is throwing odd questions at you in rapid-fire style or asking illegal questions (dealt with later in this chapter), roll with the punches, answer politely, but don't be intimidated—you are being tested under stress. Keep your cool. You have had your share of disruptive, recalcitrant students; this should be duck soup.

To sum up this section, let's borrow a word from Greek literature: *sophrosyne*, a word that means self-restraint and a sense of balance. You would do well to exhibit this trait in word, action, and dress as you prepare for and take part in the interview. After all, what you are looking for on the other side of the desk is an associate who will like you, hire you, or at least refer you to someone else. So listen to the needs, and sell your skills and competence and your ability to do the job. As a teacher you're persuasive. Try for the gold star. You'll survive the experience, and will probably enjoy it.

Responses to Avoid. There are very few responses or statements that are turnoffs to employment managers, but there are a few, such as:

"I don't know what I want to do."

If you don't, who will know? If this is still your answer, you haven't finished your preliminary homework.

"I want to work with people."

This statement sounds odd to a working professional. How can you work without working with people? Qualify your answer: "I hope there is a team effort in this department. Although I enjoy working independently, I believe that the goals of a department are accomplished more successfully on a team."

Since teachers often work independently, this conveys the message that you want and accept give-and-take, something that is very important in all occupations.

"I want to do administrative work."

Too general. Clarify: "I would like to assist in the administrative work of the purchasing department, or the editing department, where I can use my organizational and planning skills to benefit the company."

"I want to do something satisfying and creative."

Since this is everyone's goal, elaborate: "I would like to work in the audio-visual department where I can prepare slides and do film work. I enjoy creative work and have already done animated work in this field."

Questions Asked By Interviewers—And Suggested Responses

Even if you practice answering a good many questions, the interviewer may not ask you any from your list—many people have verified this possibility. The practice of preparing answers in advance can, however, get you into the thought processes of the interviewer.

Suppose you are thrown a question from left field—one that never occurred to you at all? Take your time in responding; no one will discredit you for thinking it through. In fact, if you say to the interviewer, "That's a good question. May I have a moment to think it over?" you will please him or her for having framed a good question.

Here are some questions you are likely to be asked, and some possible answers.

1. "Why are you leaving your job (or seeking a new job, or career)?"
   a. Time for a new challenge.
   b. Opportunity to apply new skills learned in recent (job-related) course work.
   c. More administrative responsibilities (related to job).
2. "Are you presently employed?"
Interviewers wonder why individuals are unemployed: should they make a job offer if no one else did?

If you are unemployed, don't answer frivolously ("I quit teaching and have been lying on a rock just to get a good suntan." That's a no-no, even if it's true.)
   a. Indicate a vigorous job hunt.
   b. Blame the times, the economy, the keen competition, but stay optimistic.
3. "What made you select this field?"
   a. State your preparation and courses.
   b. Relate qualifications, talents, and abilities. Be specific.
Never say, "I don't know" or "Joe suggested it."

4. "I've read your resume. Now, tell me about yourself, in your own words."

Don't take this opportunity to pull a soap opera scenario; keep to business.

    a. I've done so and so.

    b. I've taken such and such relevant courses.

    c. My skills in this and that field are applicable to this job.

    d. Interpersonal skills will be useful because, and so on. (Have your answers people-related as well as task-related.)

5. "Why do you want to join us?" Or, "What do you know about us?"

Never say "Not much." You should have information that you have looked up, such as:

    a. Your reputation in the community is excellent.

    b. Your growth rate has been about thirty percent a year, and I want to be part of a dynamic company.

    c. I want to work in social service and I've heard that you are doing innovative work.

6. "In what community organizations are you involved?"

This question may be a fishing expedition. In certain jobs (travel, insurance, real estate, banking, and so on), community contacts are helpful. You do not have to reveal political party or religious denomination, or anything controversial. This line of questioning may also be testing your energy level: your desire to work on committees; your civic sense; and the quality and kind of commitments you make.

7. "Do you work well under pressure?"

    a. Yes (if you do; give a short example).

    b. If you don't, get clarification from the interviewer, i.e., Why did you ask that question? If you don't work well under pressure, you certainly don't want a new job and a new ulcer. But why reveal your predilections? The question may not even be related to the job at hand. (Interviewers are human and sometimes ask questions that are irrelevant just to make conversation.)

8. "What were your major accomplishments on your last job?"

    a. Give a qualitative response: improved the scores of my classes by making pupils test-wise.

    b. Give a quantitative response: collaborated with ten urban schools in presenting a multi-ethnic exchange of ideas.

    9. "What do you expect to be doing in five years (or next year, or in ten years)?"

Avoid saying, "I don't know." Be prepared.

    a. More responsibility in the field you have chosen.

    b. Increased administrative responsibilities, management in a field you have chosen.

    c. Increased scope of work.

    d. Take courses in order to be more helpful to employer.

Tip. Do not say that you expect to move on and start another entirely different career. Personnel managers want to know that you will stay with them and expand your responsibilities as your talent increases.

    10. "Which is more important, the money or the job?"

Never minimize the importance of money. Most people work because they need the money.

    a. Money is important, but . . .

    b. The nature of the work is more important, and so on. Never stress money in the beginning unless you are entering a sales position. Salespeople *must* by motivated by the desire for money and prestige.

    11. "What do you think of your present boss? And colleagues?"

The truth of the matter is that many people change or quit their jobs because of interpersonal reasons; but don't demean your peers.

    a. I respect principal's ability to handle parents.

    b. Administrators try to support our programs even though we have budgetary restraints.

    c. Most colleagues are ambitious, creative, responsible (even if a few are lazy, uncreative, and irresponsible).

    12. "How would you feel about working for someone older? Younger? A man? A woman?"

    a. I can't foresee any difficulties.

   b. No problem; I've worked for both.

   c. I'll survive—and thrive.

13. "Tell me about yourself."

   a. I'm a happy, optimistic person who enjoys family, work, and hobbies. (Don't recite an autobiography.)

   b. I enjoy working independently but find a team more efficacious and satisfying. (Choose your style, but be positive and don't ramble on and on and on.)

14. "What are your greatest strengths?"

   a. One part of your answer should relate to accomplishments.

   b. One part of your answer should be about your ability to work well with people. They are both important.

15. "What are your weaknesses?"

Turn these answers into strengths.

   a. I am very conscientious and expect a lot from others, too—sometimes too much. But in the long run, we are all proud of the results.

   b. I have creative projects that I like to implement—too quickly. I have learned how to sell my ideas and to be more patient with implementation, however.

16. "I hope you're not one of those women's libbers."

This may or may not be put in the form of a question, but you are still expected to respond. Try to understand the motive behind the question (anti-feminist?). Watch for body language, too. Only you can decide whether you want to adjust your attitude or leave.

   a. Smile (may suffice).

   b. I take a humanistic and personal approach to each issue.

   c. I believe strongly in equality for all people. (Period. No debates.)

17. "What book are you reading now [did you last read]?"

Be prepared. Never say that you've been too busy to read. Don't worry about *what* you read. President Kennedy used to relax with mysteries. It's perfectly acceptable.

18. "I think you are overqualified for this job."

Don't just nod and agree. Ask for an explanation. Use the answer to correct the image.

    a. What do you mean by "overqualified"? (You can defend
       a point, if you can get to the heart of the question.)
    b. The employer will benefit by your additional knowl-
       edge.
    c. The job may not need all your qualifications, but in time
       the position may expand.
    d. There is a great deal that you can still learn as well as
       contribute.

Sometimes asking for a tour of the plant at this time can give you
the opportunity to establish rapport and possibly even change
the interviewer's point of view.

If at the end of the interview you have definitely been told
that "This is it, baby. Goodbye," or some such indicator, and you
are certain there's no way to counter the verdict, ask for leads;
you may be perfect for the next person. (Oh, yes, this happens!)
If it is not appropriate, or if you forget to ask for names, you can
call later on, even after you have received a "Thanks, but no
thanks" letter. Call or write, express your thanks, and request
contacts. This gesture will also keep your name before the manager. There may be a next time, so keep your association pleasant
and professional.

Questions You May Want To Ask

It is important for you, too, to ask questions, because this permits
a freer interchange of ideas and creates a more normal give-and-
take climate.

Even if you are adept at asking questions, restrain yourself
from playing Grand Inquisitor. Listen carefully to answers; they
will give you insights into the person and the institution. (Salary
questions will be discussed later on in this chapter.) Here are
some questions you may want to ask:

1. "What are the company's criteria for hiring someone in
this position?" (Skilled interviewers probably won't fall for this,
but if you can get an answer to this question early in the interview,
you will have the opportunity to link the answer with your qualifications for the job.)

2. "Is this a new position?" If it is new, you can often help to define the job, but first ask for the design that the company has in mind.

3. "What are the duties and responsibilities of the position? To whom does the person in this position report?" This will give you the opportunity to have the position clarified from the standpoint of your own needs.

4. "Is this position based on a grant or is it a permanent position?" In governmental, educational, and social service agencies there are many temporary positions that may or may not be renewed. If you are interested in the experience, the contacts, or the exposure, then a job based on grant may suit you. But if you don't want to repeat the job-search process, don't take it. Where will you be at the end of the year if it is not renewed?

5. "What is it like working for this company?" An honest question like this may open up a Pandora's box. Weigh the answers. They may provide interesting insights.

6. "What is the management's policy concerning promoting from within?" After all, the company is interviewing from the outside; why isn't it promoting someone? Maybe you won't be promoted, either.

7. "Why did the previous person leave this job?"

8. "Are there merit raises? Bonuses? At what intervals?" Sometimes salaries are not negotiable—the job pays so and so and that's that. If you want the job, the answers to these questions may help in your own decision.

Towards the end of the interview, you may want to ask questions pertaining to the interviewer's feeling about your qualifications for the position. This can provide you with valuable feedback for the next interview. But if you like the sound of the job, *ask for it.* Your positive interest could influence the interviewer.

Don't sit around waiting for the telephone to ring or for a letter to arrive in the mail. People rarely hit bingo on the basis of one interview. Sharpen your skills and make more network calls. Keep going!

After the Interview

Think it over: Do you want the job? Does the environment feel right to you? Your feelings are important.

Evaluate your performance. What improvements should you make? Did you listen too much and talk too little (or vice versa)? Were you confident? Did you try to convince the interviewer that you could do the job? Did you ask for the job?

Send a thank-you letter immediately, summing up the contribution you could make and inserting anything you may have neglected. If you were told that the interviewer's dog had a cold, inquire after its health. Call after a few days (unless you were told otherwise) and express your interest again. (A tip: if you call after 5:00 P.M., you may reach your party directly; secretaries usually leave promptly at 5:00.)

"Won't I bother the interviewer if I call?" teachers ask. The answer: The interviewer will think you're not interested if you don't. Your call could cut through a lot of red tape. If you're interested, call.

Illegal Questions

Every state has laws against discrimination based on race, color, age, nationality, marital status, and sex. Don't assume that everyone is aware of the rules. Both employment interviewers and employment applications will probably ask loaded questions. The person seeking employment is often in a bind. If you refuse to fill out or answer questions, you may set up an antagonism right from the start. The other party may not even be aware of the reasons for your anger or embarrassment. If you feel it is unnecessary to answer questions, don't. Leave them blank. Verbal questions—like "How old are you?"—may be countered politely and with firm dignity: "Does the answer pertain to my ability to do the job? I'm very energetic and would enjoy every phase of this job." Maintain your position and your confidence. Here are some of these loaded questions:

- Are you married or divorced?
- How old are your children?

Sample Letter Following the Interview

14621 Stanford Place
Encino, California 91316
(213) 555-7774

April 11, 1985

Mr. Irma Nowell
Personnel Director
Holland Associates
24632 Homewood Way
Encino, California 91316

Dear Irma,

I enjoyed our meeting very much and want to express my appreciation for your courtesy.

The position of training specialist at Holland Associates is particularly appealing in that I will be able to use my experience in career development at the same time I learn management techniques from John. Please thank him for his courtesy during my interview. I would be very pleased to work with him.

Because it will be difficult to reach me at work, I will call you on Monday. I am eager to meet with you again.

Sincerely,

Mario Rossi

Mario Rossi

- Where does your husband work?
- This is very hard work. How will you manage? (at your age?)
- What is your date of birth?
- How long have you been out of school?
- Do you have a disability? (It is legal to add: "that would hinder you in this position.")
- How old are you?
- Is it "Miss" or "Mrs."?
- Are you planning to have children? When?
- Do you have a boyfriend? Are you planning to leave us soon in order to get married?
- Do you have any outstanding debts? Can we do a credit check on you?
- What was your parents' country of origin?

You can see how personal questions can be used directly or indirectly to obtain facts about your private life.

If you are certain that you were discriminated against, contact the Equal Employment Opportunity Commission in your state, or EEOC, 1800 G Street, Washington, DC 20596.

About Salary

Stage One: Testing the Water. At the first interview you may be asked about the salary you are requesting. Although you may ask the interviewer, "What is the salary for this position?" or "What is the salary range for this position?" not all personnel people will respond; they want to know the salary that is *acceptable* to you. So you can see that the burden is on *you* to know the salary range for the particular job you are seeking.

If you are called back for a second interview—and only serious contenders for positions are asked to return—you may need to know how to *negotiate* salary, a somewhat different technique but a key component in job strategy.

Here are a few methods of finding the information you need on the salary range for the position, if it is not listed in this book:

- Look in the employment ads of the Sunday newspaper.
- Call one of the management consultants listed in the newspaper. They tend to advertise for experienced people, so ask them the rate for entry-level positions.
- Ask the personnel department directly. (It pays to take a few personnel people out to lunch, if you become friendly. In industry, individuals' salaries are a taboo topic, but a friendship can often provide you with salary ranges.) If a particular range is from $18,000 to $22,000, the less-experienced would probably receive the lower end of the range. In the public sector, salaries are more readily available, upon request, than in the private sector (business).
- Look in the *Occupational Outlook Handbook.* (Salaries are usually outdated even before the book goes to press, so tack on about eight percent a year, the average per annum increase, for every year since the book was published.)
- Check career center job listings; they often include salary.
- Call or visit the nearest Employment Service Office.
- Ask a friend in the field.

As a career changer, you must decide upon the lowest salary you would be willing to accept. Only you can determine your needs. If you wish to test the receptivity to your credentials and the reality of your worth, the interview should provide that opportunity. You can always adjust your answer later, if you must.

It is strongly recommended that you put off salary questions until you think you have convinced the interviewer of your qualifications and have established good rapport. Some interviewers will be very direct: "How much are you earning?" Try to put them off with this kind of a response: "Salary is important, but the responsibility that goes along with this position is what interests me most. Would you please describe the level of responsibility?"

By asking questions, you are buying time to convince the manager of your ability to do the job and your confidence in that ability. Salary statements made too early may eliminate you, especially under these circumstances:

- If your present salary is too high.
- If your salary is higher than that of the person to whom you will report.
- If you appear to be overqualified (whatever that means).
- If you appear at first to be underqualified.
- If your present salary or job status is too low. Conversation can buy the time to be convincing.

Let's look at the questions from both sides of the table, assuming that now we're ready to answer them.

"What salary are you earning now?"

If you are earning $26,000 as an experienced teacher and the job pays from $20,000 to $24,000, you may be judged to be overqualified. As a general rule, industry does not respect someone who is willing to accept a lower salary. On the other hand, if you are unemployed or earning much less, the company will be hard pressed to find valid reasons for paying well over your present level. *You must counter any remarks with cogent reasons to hire you,* such as:

- I will be more valuable to your company because I bring maturity and directly related skills.
- I have excellent recommendations I can show you. Here they are.
- I believe that I should receive a higher salary because of my previous experience.
- Career changers must be realistic about lower salaries at first.
- I have a *strong* desire to join your particular firm because its reputation is legendary.

If you are asked, "How much money would you accept?", you must be prepared to answer, but don't think that this is necessarily a job offer (misunderstanding this has caused hardships, in some classic cases). Interviewers ask rhetorical questions just to make conversation. If the question of salary does not arise, it is perfectly acceptable for you to bring up the topic, with discretion.

Don't get discouraged if a job offer is not made. There are many reasons that candidates do not receive job offers. Your resume may have looked appealing but, after consideration, the company may decide to promote someone from within, a very common practice. Keep going; just regard each interview as a dress rehearsal for the next one!

Stage Two: Negotiation. Teachers are very much concerned about this aspect of an interview. Let me preface my view of the process with a family story that may add levity to the situation.

My daughter, at age nineteen, was an expert at negotiating an hourly rate for summer jobs held during her college days. Both her parents had coached her in the "art of winning at the bargaining table." Her skill was aided immeasurably by the considerable personal and persuasive powers she possessed. She knew that the art of negotiation was a game and she learned how to play it very well, often with humorous results. When she was offered an hourly rate, regardless of the figure, she would use body language to express her displeasure: a sad look here and a furrowed brow there could get her a twenty-five or fifty cent hourly raise before she even used her verbal ability! With one employer she was particularly persuasive, and she was told that she was "fancy with the footwork." Although the meaning of the expression was unknown to her, and she wasn't certain whether the remark was meant as an insult or a compliment, she took the job—the price was right.

This story is an introduction to a process that is not as difficult as it may seem to the novice negotiator. Teachers have often had little or no experience with this topic, since the pay scale in public school systems is predetermined. A beginning teacher starts at the bottom rung and then receives increments, cost of living increases, and merit raises through established channels. Most salary negotiation is done for the teacher by the union. If you are interviewing for a teaching job, however, there are certain situations that may permit limited negotiation, as in the following cases:

- An experienced teacher may be able to negotiate for a certain level appropriate to the situation.
- A former teacher may be reentering the field and may request a higher salary as compensation for volunteer work

during his or her absence or for substitute or related part-time work.

- A beginning teacher may wish to include experience as a substitute teacher.
- A mature adult, either as a career changer or as a recent graduate, may be able to cite life experience or previous work experience.
- A candidate with a specific expertise—that is, a statesman or a plumber entering, respectively, a university or a vocational school—might negotiate (and would, ironically, probably receive a lower salary).
- A teacher with a rare or badly-needed skill (for example, a teacher of tuba) may be successful in requesting a higher salary—if aware of his or her unique position.

In all cases, if the opportunity seems open to negotiations during an interview, don't back down. There is no risk, because the process takes place only near the end of the interview when both parties are certain of mutual consent. Don't sell yourself short. Many men and women do, especially if they are unemployed or eager to get a foot in the door. A low starting salary can take a year or more to make up.

What factors can be brought into play as bargaining points?

Life experience; graduate credits; substitute work; experience as a parent or spouse; experience coaching a team or leading a workshop; previous work experience; political activity; age; personal or family needs (divorce, college-age children, disabled child); distance to work; volunteer positions; and relocation. Companies do take human needs into consideration, if their salary structure permits flexibility.

And of course another factor that always helps is knowing the interviewer, or interviewing with an officer of a small company; the latter not only has clout but has a good understanding of the value of an employee.

What is the negotiating scenario like?

There is no formula; it is, instead, a game of brinksmanship that is played more or less in this manner:

Interviewer: I can offer you $20,000 in this position. [You know that the going rate is $24,000.]

Applicant [frowning]: You know that I like the job, but I have a child whom I have to send to a special school [or you live fifty miles away, and so on; leave out your "need" for a Mercedes] and this would be difficult to accomplish on that salary. [Pause, frown.]

Interviewer: How much do you need?

Applicant: [Rule: Always start high.] I was hoping to start at $24,000; I'll be using up more gas getting here, too.

Interviewer: The best I can do is $22,000. [Interviewer had this in mind all along, so he's satisfied.]

Applicant: Great, Thanks a lot; I appreciate your thoughtfulness. [Didn't expect more than $20,000.]

Interviewer: How soon can you start?

In its most simplified form, this is the give-and-take of negotiating. There are different kinds of scenarios and they don't always work. For instance, the scenario above could end this way:

Applicant: $20,000 is low because . . . [as above.]

Interviewer: Sorry, that is the best I can do.

Applicant: I really am eager to assume the responsibilities of this job. How soon could my salary be reviewed if I accepted?

Interviewer: I can't make special rules. I'm afraid that you'd have to wait a year. (Or: We can review your salary after six months.)

Applicant: Jim, you know I'm hooked. When do I begin?

You are still a winner because you wouldn't have gone this far if you hadn't already decided that this was the job you wanted.

A higher-level applicant has more opportunity to say, "I'm sorry, I cannot take this position without a twenty percent increase." But teachers who are changing careers will have to be expert negotiators to play the "call me if you change your mind" game that is played successfully at higher levels.

There are often benefits companies give to their employees that are very substantial. Often, they add up to a third of the salary, in addition to the dollars received! So be certain to inquire about benefits. They vary, and can add a goodly sum onto your income. What items are paid for? Fully? What is the employee contribution to benefit plans? Is there profit-sharing? How much in profit-sharing was paid out last year to each employee? The year before? What about retirement plans? Educational benefits? Bonuses? Life insurance? Extras?

You can see that the differences can be substantial. Don't avoid doing your arithmetic; all these items add up.

At the negotiating stage, if you find that the salary, the person to whom you would report, or any other conditions just don't feel right, should you still continue to negotiate? Yes, but you should change the script. You have every right to ask the interviewer for a day or even a week (he or she may even agree on more time) in which to speak to your family or to think it over in your leisure. Will the company select someone else in the meantime? No, that is unethical. A bona fide offer is like an unwritten contract. If possible, have the company send a letter of confirmation to you; this is common practice. At any rate, sleeping on an offer is usual and makes good sense. Changing your mind is also an option. If you sleep on an offer and find that you have a nightmare, call and say, "Thanks, but no thanks." Better now than later.

After all is said and done, remember, you need only one job. Get ready, get set, and go out and seek it!

Appendix

Private Industry Addresses

American Society for Training and Development
P.O. Box 5307
Madison, WI 53705
(608) 274–3440

National Alliance of Businessmen
(There are ten regional offices of this organization, as well as offices
in many cities. Check your telephone directory.)

Educational Associations

Adult Education Association of the U.S.A.
810 Eighteenth Street, N.W.
Washington, DC 20006
(202) 347–9574

Association of Independent Colleges and Schools
1730 M Street, N.W.
Washington, DC 20036
(202) 659–2460

American Association of Junior Colleges
One Dupont Circle
Washington, DC 20009

Association for Supervision and Curriculum Development (ASCD)
1701 K Street, N.W.
Washington, DC 20006

National Association of Trade and Technical Schools
2021 L Street, N.W.
Washington, DC 20036
(202) 296–8892

U.S. Government

United States Department of Education
Office of the Assistant Secretary for Educational Research and Improvement
National Center for Education Statistics
Washington, DC 20202

Other Associations

National Trade and Professional Associations of the United States.
Columbia Books Inc., 777 14th Street, N.W., Suite 1334, Washington, DC 20011

Gale's Encyclopedia of Associations. Gale Research Company, Book Tower, Detroit, MI 48226

Association Management, monthly magazine of the American Society of Association Executives, 1575 Eye Street, N.W., Washington, DC 20005

ESANE, Box 288, Weston, MA 02193

Most Recent Addresses of State Employment Offices

Alabama. Department of Industrial Relations, 649 Monroe St., Montgomery 36130; (205) 832–3626
Alaska. Employment Security Division, Department of Labor, 1111 W. 8th Ave., P.O. Box 3-7000, Juneau 99811; (907) 465–2714
Arizona. Department of Economic Security, P.O. Box 6123, Phoenix 85005; (602) 271–4900
Arkansas. Employment Security Division, Department of Labor, P.O. Box 2981, Little Rock 72203; (501) 371–2121
California. Employment Development Department, 800 Capitol Mall, Sacramento 95814; (916) 445–9212
Colorado. Division of Employment and Training, Department of Labor & Employment, 251 E. 12th Ave., Denver 80203; (303) 893–2400
Connecticut. Employment Security Division, Connecticut Labor Department, 200 Folloy Brook Blvd., Wethersfield 06109; (203) 566–4280
Delaware. Department of Labor, 820 N. French St., Wilmington 19801; (302) 571–2710

District of Columbia. Department of Employment Services, 500 C St., NW,/District Unemployment Compensation Board, 6th & Pennsylvania Ave., NW, Washington, DC 20001; (202) 724–3928

Florida. Division of Employment Security, Department of Labor & Employment Security, 2590 Executive Ctr. Circle E., Suite 206, Tallahassee 32301; (904) 488–3104

Georgia. Employment Security Agency, Department of Labor, State Labor Bldg., 254 Washington St., SW, Atlanta 30334; (404) 656–3014

Guam. Department of Labor, Government of Guam, P.O. Box 2950, Agana 96910

Hawaii. Department of Labor and Industrial Relations, 830 Punchbowl St., Honolulu 96813; (808) 548–3150

Idaho. Department of Employment, P.O. Box 35, Boise 83735; (208) 384–2731

Illinois. Bureau of Employment Security, Department of Labor, 910 S. Michigan Ave., Chicago 60605; (312) 793–3500

Indiana. Employment Security Division, 10 N. Senate Ave., Indianapolis; (317) 633–7670

Iowa. Department of Job Service, 1000 E. Grand Ave., Des Moines 50319; (515) 281–5361

Kansas. Division of Employment, Department of Human Resources, 401 Topeka Ave., Topeka 66603; (913) 296–5000

Kentucky. Bureau for Manpower Services, Department for Human Resources, 275 E. Main St., Frankfort 40621; (502) 564–7130

Louisiana. Office of Employment Security, Department of Labor, P.O. Box 44094, Baton Rouge 70804; (504) 387–2192

Maine. Bureau of Employment Security, Department of Manpower Affairs, 20 Union St., P.O. Box 309, Augusta 04330; (207) 289–3814

Maryland. Employment Security Administration, Department of Human Resources, State Office Bldg., 1100 N. Eutaw St., Baltimore 21201; (301) 383–5070

Massachusetts. Division of Employment Security, Charles F. Hurley ES Bldg., Boston 02114; (617) 727–6600

Michigan. Employment Security Commission, 7310 Woodward Ave., Detroit 48202; (313) 876–5000

Minnesota. Department of Economic Security, 390 N. Robert St., St. Paul 55101; (612) 296–3711

Mississippi. Employment Security Commission, 1520 W. Capital St., P.O. Box 1699, Jackson 39205; (601) 354–8711

Missouri. Division of Employment Security, Department of Labor & Industrial Relations, 421 E. Dunklin St., P.O. Box 59, Jefferson City 65101; (314) 751–3215

Montana. Employment Security Division of Montana, Department of Labor & Industry, P.O. Box 1728, Helena 59624; (406) 449–3662

Nebraska. Division of Employment, Department of Labor, 94600 State House Station, Lincoln 68509; (402) 475–8451

Nevada. Employment Security Department, 500 E. 3rd St., Carson City 89713; (702) 885–4635

New Hampshire. Department of Employment Security, 32 S. Main St., Room 204, Concord 03301; (603) 224–3311

New Jersey. Division of Employment Services, Department of Labor & Industry, C.N. 110, Trenton 08625; (609) 292–2323

New Mexico. Employment Security Department, P.O. Box 1928, Albuquerque 87103; (505) 842–3239

New York. Department of Labor, State Campus Building 12, Albany 12240; (518) 457–2471

North Carolina. Employment Security Commission of North Carolina, 200 W. Jones St., P.O. Box 25903, Raleigh 27611; (919) 829–7546

North Dakota. Job Service North Dakota, 1000 E. Divide Ave., P.O. Box 1537, Bismark; (701) 224–2837

Ohio. Bureau of Employment Services, 145 S. Front St., Columbus 43215; (614) 466–2100

Oklahoma. Employment Security Commission, 200 Will Rogers Memorial Office Bldg., Oklahoma City 73105; (405) 521–3794

Oregon. Employment Division, Department of Human Resources, 875 Union St., NE, Salem 97311; (503) 378–3211

Pennsylvania. Office of Employment Security, Department of Labor & Industry, P.O. Box 1899, Harrisburg 17105; (717) 787–6223

Puerto Rico. Bureau of Employment Security, Department of Labor & Human Resources, 505 Munoz Rivera Ave., Hato Rey 00918; (809) 765–3570

Rhode Island. Department of Employment Security, 24 Mason St., Providence 02903; (401) 277–3732

South Carolina. Employment Security Commission, 1550 Gadsden St., P.O. Box 995, Columbia 29202; (803) 758–2686

South Dakota. Department of Labor, 700 N. Illinois, Pierre 57501; (605) 224–3101

Tennessee. Department of Employment Security, Cordell Hull State Office Bldg., Nashville 37219; (615) 741–2131

Texas. Employment Commission, 638 TEC Bldg. 15th & Congress Ave., Austin 78778; (512) 472–6251

Utah. Department of Employment Security, 174 Social Hall Ave., P.O. Box 11249, Salt Lake City 84147; (801) 533–2201

Vermont. Department of Employment Security, Green Mountain Dr., P.O. Box 488, Montpelier 05602; (802) 229–0311

Virginia. Employment Commission, Department of Labor and Industry, 703 E. Main St., P.O. Box 1358, Richmond 23211; (804) 786–3001

Virgin Islands. Employment Security Agency, 35 Norre Gade St., P.O. Box 1090, Charlotte Amalie 00801

Washington. Employment Security Department, P.O. Box 367, Olympia 98504; (206) 753–5114

West Virginia. Department of Employment Security, 112 California Ave., Charleston 25305; (304) 348–2630

Wisconsin. Job Service, Wisconsin Department of Industry, Labor & Human Relations, P.O. Box 7946, Madison 53707; (608) 266–7074

Wyoming. Employment Security Commission of Wyoming, P.O. Box 2760, Casper 82602; (307) 237–3701

Bibliography

Education

Boyer, Ernest. *High School: A Report on Secondary Education in America.* Princeton, NJ: Carnegie Foundation for the Advancement of Teaching, 1983.

Cusick, Philip. *The American High School and the Egalitarian Ideal.* New York: Longman, 1983.

Feistritzer, Emily C. *The Condition of Teaching: A State by State Analysis.* Princeton, NJ: Carnegie Foundation for the Advancement of Teaching, 1983.

Goodlad, John I. *A Place Called School: Prospects for the Future.* New York: McGraw-Hill, 1983.

Lasch, Christopher. *The Culture of Narcissism.* New York: W.W. Norton, 1979.

Lightfoot, Sara Lawrence. *The Good High School: Portraits of Culture and Character.* New York: Basic Books, 1983.

The National Commission on Excellence in Education. *A Nation at Risk: The Imperative for Educational Reform.* Washington, DC: U.S. Department of Education, 1983.

The National Science Board Commission on Precollege Education in Mathematics, Science, and Technology. *Educating Americans for the 21st Century.* 2 vols. Washington, DC: National Science Foundation, 1983.

Peters, Thomas J., and Robert Waterman, II. *In Search of Excellence: Lessons from America's Best Run Companies.* New York: Harper & Row, 1982.

Ravitch, Diane. *The Troubled Crusade: American Education 1945–1980.* New York: Basic Books, 1983.

Sizer, Theodore R. *Horace's Compromise: The Dilemma of the American High School.* Boston: Houghton Mifflin, 1984.

Task Force of the Business Higher Education Forum. *America: Competitive Challenge: The Need for a National Response.* Washington, DC: Business Higher Education Forum, 1983.

Task Force on Education for Economic Growth. *Action for Excellence: A Comprehensive Plan to Improve Our Nation's Schools.* Denver: Education Commission of the States, 1983.

The Twentieth Century Fund Task Force on Federal Elementary and Secondary Education Policy. *Making the Grade.* New York: Twentieth Century Fund, 1983.

Reference Works in Education

Bailey, Janet. *The El-Hi Market 1984–89,* Knowledge Industry Publications, Inc., 701 Westchester Avenue, White Plains, NY 10604

Broadcasting/Cable Yearbook 1983/84. Broadcasting Publishers, Inc., Washington, DC

Micro-Computer Hardware and Software in the El-Hi Market 1983–87, by the editors of Knowledge Industry Publications, Inc.

National Association of State Approved Colleges and Universities, Inc. *Directory of United States Traditional and Alternative Colleges and Universities, 1984–1986.* NASACU, 3843 Massachusetts Avenue, N.W., Washington, DC 20016

Projections of Education Statistics to 1985–86, National Center for Educational Statistics, U.S. Department of Health, Education, and Welfare

Business Reference Books

Directory of American Savings and Loan Associations: The Complete Directory. 29th ed. Baltimore: T.K. Sanderson, 1983.

Directory of Manufacturers. Boston: George D. Hall Company, 1983.

Directory of Special Libraries in U.S.A. and Canada. 8th ed. vols 1 and 2. Brigitte Darney, ed. Detroit: Gale Research, 1983.

Encyclopedia of Associations. 18th ed. vol. 1 1983, vol. 2 1984. Denise S. Akey, ed. Detroit: Gale Research, 1983 and 1984.

Million Dollar Directory. 3 vols. New York: Standard & Poors Corp., 1984.

Standard & Poors Corp. *Standard & Poors Register of Corporations, Directors and Executives.* New York: Standard & Poors Corp., 1984.

Careers—General

Adams, Robert Lang, ed. *The Boston Job Bank: A Comprehensive Guide to Major Employers Throughout Greater Boston.* 2nd ed. (Job Bank Series). Brighton, MA: Bob Adams, Inc., 1983.

Albrecht, Maryann, and Helene Seiten. *Growing: A Woman's Guide to Career Satisfaction.* Scottsdale, AZ: Lifeline Learning, 1980.

Arnold, John D. *Trading Up: A Career Guide.* New York: Doubleday, 1984.

Beard, Marna L., and Michael J. McGahey. *Alternative Careers for Teachers.* New York: Arco, 1983.

Bestor, Dorothy. *Aside from Teaching, What in the World Can You Do?* Seattle: University of Washington Press, 1982.

Bolles, Richard N. *The Quick Job-Hunting Map.* Berkeley, CA: Ten Speed Press, 1982.

——————. *The Three Boxes of Life and How to Get Out of Them.* Berkeley, CA: Ten Speed Press, 1981.

——————. *What Color is Your Parachute?* Rev. ed. Berkeley, CA: Ten Speed Press, 1983.

Boyd, Kathleen, *et al. Career Connections: A Guide to Career Planning Services Throughout Massachusetts.* Brighton, MA: Bob Adams, Inc., 1983.

Catalyst Staff. *Marketing Yourself.* New York: Bantam, 1981.

——————. *Upward Mobility.* New York: Holt, Rinehart and Winston, 1983.

——————. *What to Do With the Rest of Your Life.* New York: Simon and Schuster, 1980.

Chronicle Career Index Annual. Rev. ed. Moravia, NY: Chronicle Guidance Publications, Inc., 1983.

The College Blue Book. Vol. 5: *Occupational Education*. 18th ed. New York: Macmillan, 1981.

Cowle, Jerry. *How to Survive Getting Fired—and Win*. New York: Warner Books, 1980.

Crystal, John C., and Richard N. Bolles. *Where Do I Go From Here With My Life?* Berkeley, CA: Ten Speed Press, 1980.

Davenport, Rita. *Making Time, Making Money: A Step-by-Step Program for Setting Your Goals and Achieving Success*. New York: St. Martin's Press, 1982.

Deutsch, Arnold R. *The Complete Job Book*. New York: Cornerstone Library, 1980.

Dun's Employment Opportunities Directory: The Career Guide 1983/1984. Parsippany, NJ: Dun & Bradstreet, Inc., 1983.

Egelston, Roberta Riethmiller. *Career Planning Materials: A Guide to Sources and Their Use*. Chicago: American Library Assoc., 1981.

Eichenbaum, Louise, and Susie Orbach. *What Do Women Want?* New York: Coward-McCann, 1983.

Figler, Howard. *The Complete Job-Search Handbook: All the Skills You Need to Get Any Job and Have a Good Time Doing It*. New York: Holt, Rinehart and Winston, 1980.

Gale, Barry, and Linda Gale. *Discover What You're Best At: The National Career Aptitude Test*. New York: Simon and Schuster, 1982.

Germann, Richard, and Peter Arnold. *Bernard Haldane Associates' Job and Career Building*. Berkeley, CA: Ten Speed Press, 1980.

Goodman, Leonard. *Alternative Careers for Teachers, Librarians, and Counselors*. New York: Monarch Press, 1982.

Goodman, Leonard H., comp. *Current Career and Occupational Literature*. New York: H.W. Wilson, 1982.

Greiff, Barrie S., and Preston K. Munter. *Trade-Offs: Executive, Family and Organizational Life*. New York: New American Library, 1980.

Haldane, Bernard. *Career Satisfaction and Success: How to Know and Manage Your Strengths*. Rev. ed. New York: AMACOM, 1982.

Harragan, Betty L. *Knowing the Score: Play-by-Play Directions for Women on the Job*. New York: St. Martin's Press, 1983.

Hennig, Margaret, and Ann Jardim. *The Managerial Woman*. New York: Anchor, 1981.

Ireland, LaVerne H. *The Teacher's & Librarian's Alternative Job Hunt Helper: An Annotated List of Transferable Job Skills and Alternative Career Possibilities*. Davis, CA: Petervin Press, 1984.

Jackson, Tom. *Guerilla Tactics in the Job Market.* New York: Bantam, 1982.

Jackson, Tom, and Davidyne Mayleas. *The Hidden Job Market for the Eighties.* New York: New York Times Book Co., 1981.

Kaye, Beverly L. *Up is Not the Only Way: A Guide for Career Development Practitioners.* Englewood Cliffs, NJ: Prentice-Hall, 1982.

Kline, Linda, and Lloyd Feinstein. *Career Changing: The Worry-Free Guide.* Boston: Little, Brown, 1982.

Krumboltz, John D., and Daniel A. Hamel. *Assessing Career Development.* Palo Alto, CA: Mayfield Pub., 1982.

Lichty, Jacqueline. *The Educator's Job Change Manual.* Troy, MI: Phoenix Services, 1981.

Lovejoy, Clarence. *Lovejoy's Career and Vocational School Guide: A Source Book, Clue Book and Directory of Institutions Training for Job Opportunities.* 6th ed. New York: Simon and Schuster, 1982.

McBurney, William J., Jr. *Where the Jobs Are.* Radnor, PA: Chilton, 1980.

Martin, Phyllis. *Martin's Magic Formula for Getting the Right Job.* New York: St. Martin's Press, 1981.

Miller, Jean M., and Georgianna M. Dickinson. *When Apples Ain't Enough: Career Change Techniques for Teachers, Counselors and Librarians.* Sacramento, CA: Jalmar Press, 1980.

Munschauer, John L. *Jobs for English Majors and Other Smart People.* Princeton, NJ: Peterson's Guides, Inc., 1981.

Norback, Craig, ed. *Careers Encyclopedia.* Homewood, IL: Dow Jones–Irwin, 1980.

Pilder, Richard J., and William F. Pilder. *How to Find Your Life's Work: Staying Out of Traps and Taking Control of Your Career.* Englewood Cliffs, NJ: Prentice-Hall, 1981.

Powell, James. *The Prentice-Hall Global Employment Guide.* Englewood Cliffs, NJ: Prentice-Hall, 1983.

Ruyle, Gene. *Making a Life: Career Choices and the Life Process.* New York: Seabury, 1983.

Sellan, Betty-Carol. *What Can You Do With a Library Degree?* Syracuse, NY: Gaylord Professional Publications, 1980.

Thain, Richard J. *The Mid-Career Manual: A Guide to Making Smart Decisions for Your High Earning Years.* Englewood Cliffs, NJ: Prentice-Hall, 1982.

Transition from Public Service Employment to Unsubsidized Jobs in the Public and Private Sectors. Policy Research Project Report Series, No. 37. Austin, TX: L.B.J. School of Public Affairs, 1981.

U.S. Department of Labor. Bureau of Labor Statistics. *The Occupational Outlook Handbook.* Biennial. 1979–1982.

——————————. *The Occupational Outlook Quarterly.*

Wright, John W. *The American Almanac of Jobs and Salaries.* New York: Avon, 1984.

Yankelovich, Daniel. *New Rules: Searching for Self-Fulfillment in a World Turned Upside Down.* New York: Random House, 1981; Bantam, 1982.

Yeomans, William N. *Jobs 1982–1983.* New York: Putnam, 1982.

Accounting Careers

Edwards, James D., and Lynn Bergold. *Career Accounting.* Homewood, IL: Richard D. Irwin, Inc., 1981.

Felix, James V. *Accounting Career Strategies: The Comprehensive Career Planning Guide for Accounting and Financial Professionals.* Edina, MN: Career Planning Publications, 1982.

Half, Robert. *Robert Half's Success Guide for Accountants.* New York: McGraw-Hill, 1984.

Arts–Performing and Visual

Beverly Hills Bar Association and Barristers Committee for the Arts. *Visual Artists Manual: A Practical Guide to Your Career.* New York: Doubleday, 1984.

Crawford, Tad, and Arie Kopelman. *Selling Your Graphic Design and Illustration.* New York: St. Martin's Press, 1981.

Kopelman, Arie, and Tad Crawford. *Selling Your Photography.* New York: St. Martin's Press, 1980.

Reed, Maxine K., and Robert M. Reed. *Career Opportunities in Television.* New York: Facts on File, 1982.

Vahl, Rod. *Exploring Careers in Broadcast Journalism.* New York: Rosen Publishing Group, 1983.

Business Careers

Dun & Bradstreet. *America's Corporate Families: The Billion Dollar Directory, 1983.* Parsippany, NJ: Dun & Bradstreet, 1982.

Encyclopedia of Associations, National Organizations of the United States. Detroit: Gale Research, 1982.

Fields, Daisy. *A Woman's Guide to Moving Up in Business Government.* Englewood Cliffs, NJ: Prentice-Hall, 1983.

Figueroa, Oscar, and Charles Winkler. *A Business Information Guidebook.* New York: AMACOM, 1980.

Flumiani, Carlo M. *The Technical Wall Street Encyclopedia.* Albuquerque, NM: Institute for Economic and Financial Research, 1982.

How to Find Information About Companies. Washington, DC: Washington Researchers, 1983.

Mainstream Access, Inc. *The Banking Job Finder.* Englewood Cliffs, NJ: Prentice-Hall, 1981.

――――――――――. *The Energy Job Finder.* Englewood Cliffs, NJ: Prentice-Hall, 1981.

Standard and Poor's. *Standard and Poor's Register of Corporations, Directors and Executives.* 3 vol. New York: Standard and Poor's, 1983.

Wasserman, Paul. *Encyclopedia of Business Information Sources.* 4th ed. Detroit: Gale Research, 1980.

Computer Careers

Carron, L. Peter, Jr. *Computers: How to Break into the Field.* Cockeysville, MD: Liberty Pub., 1982.

Consumer Guide Editors. *Computer Careers: Where the Jobs Are and How to Get Them.* New York: Fawcett, 1981.

Grundfest, Sandra, ed. *Peterson's Guide to Engineering, Science and Computer Jobs, 1984.* Princeton, NJ: Peterson's Guides, 1983.

Hsaio, T.C. *Directory of Computer Education and Research.* Latham, NY: Science and Technology Press, 1983.

Kennedy, Joyce L., and Connie Winkler. *Computer Careers: The Complete Pocket Guide to America's Fastest-Growing Job Market.* Rockville, MD: Sun Features, 1983.

McGehee, Brad M., ed. *Programmer's Market, 1984.* Cincinnati, OH: Writer's Digest, 1983.

Mainstream Access, Inc. *The Data Processing/Information Technology Job Finder.* Englewood Cliffs, NJ: Prentice-Hall, 1981.

Muller, Peter. *The Fast Track to the Top Jobs in Computer Careers.* (Fast Track Guides to Successful Careers Series). New York: Putnam Publishing Group, 1983.

Sharp, Angela. *Working with Computers.* New York: State Mutual Books, 1982.

Weintraub, Joseph S. *Exploring Careers in the Computer Field.* (Careers in Depth Series). New York: Rosen Group, 1983.

Willis, Jerry. *Computers, Teachers and Learning.* Beaverton, OR: Dilithium Press, 1983.

Federal Government Employment

Brownson, Charles P. *Federal Staff Directory, 1983–1984.* 3rd. ed. Mt. Vernon, VA: Congressional Staff Directory, 1984.

Uleck, Ronald B., ed. *Federal Career Directory.* Rev. Ed. Gaithersburg, MD: Prospect Press, 1981.

Young, Joseph, and Lucille Young. *Federal Employees' Almanac.* Merrifield, VA: Federal Employees News Digest, 1982.

Foreign Employment

Bajkai, Louis A., ed. *Teachers' Guide to Overseas Teaching: A Complete and Comprehensive Guide of English-Language Schools and Colleges Overseas.* 3rd ed. San Diego: Friends of World Teaching, 1983.

Garraty, John A., *et al.*, eds. *The New Guide to Study Abroad, 1981–1982.* New York: Harper & Row, 1980.

Griffith, Susan, *Work Your Way Around the World.* Cincinnati, OH: Writer's Digest, 1983.

Woodworth, David, ed. *Overseas Summer Jobs 1984.* Cincinnati, OH: Writer's Digest, 1983.

Health Careers

Allen, Anne S. *Introduction to the Health Professions.* 3rd ed. St. Louis: C.V. Mosby, Co., 1980.

Wischnitzer, Saul. *Barron's Guide to Medical, Dental and Allied Health Careers.* Rev. ed. Woodbury, NY: Barron's Educational Series, 1982.

Insurance Careers

Ford, Curtis B. *How to Establish an Estate Analysis Practice.* 2nd ed. Cincinnati, OH: National Underwriter, 1982.

Mainstream Access, Inc. *The Insurance Job Finder.* Englewood Cliffs, NJ: Prentice-Hall, 1982.

Paralegal Careers

Berkey, Rachel L. *New Career Opportunities in the Paralegal Profession.* New York: Arco, 1983.

Statsky, William P. *Introduction to Paralegalism: Perspectives, Problems, and Skills.* (Paralegal Series) St. Paul, MN: West Pub., 1982.

Personnel Management

Crane, Donald P. *Personnel: The Management of Human Resources.* 3rd ed. Boston: Kent Pub. Co., 1982.

Hayes, Steven W., and T. Zane Reeves. *Personnel Management in the Public Sector.* Newton, MA: Allyn & Bacon, 1984.

Karlins, Marvin. *The Human Use of Human Resources.* New York: McGraw-Hill, 1981.

Middlemist, R. Dennis, and Michael A. Hill. *Personnel Management: Jobs, People & Logic.* Englewood Cliffs, NJ: Prentice-Hall, 1983.

Public Relations

Hart, Norman, and Gilbert Lamb. *A Career in Marketing, Advertising and Public Relations.* New York: State Mutual Books, 1981.

Mainstream Access, Inc. *The Public Relations Job Finder.* Englewood Cliffs, NJ: Prentice-Hall, 1981.

Publishing Careers

Applebaum, Judith, and Nancy Evans. *How to Get Happily Published: A Complete and Candid Guide.* New York: New American Library, 1982.

Blaufox, Janice, ed. *Literary Market Place; With Names and Numbers.* 40th ed. New York: Bowker, 1981.

Mainstream Access, Inc. *The Publishing Job Finder.* Englewood Cliffs, NJ: Prentice-Hall, 1981.

Scherman, William. *How to Get the Right Job in Publishing.* Chicago: Contemporary Books, 1983.

Real Estate Careers

Bates, Dorothy R. *How to Run a Real Estate Office.* Reston, VA: Reston Pub. Co., 1981.

Mainstream Access, Inc. *The Real Estate Job Finder.* Englewood Cliffs, NJ: Prentice-Hall, 1981.

Pivar, William H. *The Real Estate Career Guide.* New York: Arco, 1980.

Poston, H.L. *Surviving and Succeeding in Real Estate.* Englewood Cliffs, NJ: Prentice-Hall, 1982.

Sales Careers

Cleaver, Clair M. *Step into Sales.* New York: Avon, 1983.

Hyatt, Carole. *The Women's Selling Game: How to Sell Yourself and Anything Else.* New York: Warner Books, 1981.

Kievman, Beverly. *The Complete Success Workbook for Today's Sales-woman.* Englewood Cliffs, NJ: Prentice-Hall, 1982.

King, David, and Karen Levine. *The Best Way in the World for a Woman to Make Money: Selling.* New York: Warner Books, 1980.

Shinn, G. *Introduction to Professional Selling.* New York: McGraw-Hill, 1982.

Siegal, Connie McClung. *Sales: The Fast Track for Women.* New York: Macmillan, 1982.

Self-Employment and Home-Based Businesses

Anderson, J.W. *Best of Both Worlds—A Guide to Home-Based Careers.* Stockbridge, MA: Berkshire Traveller, 1982.

Faux, Marian. *Successful Free-Lancing: The Complete Guide to Establishing and Running Any Kind of Free-Lance Business.* New York: St. Martin's Press, 1982.

Hewes, Jeremy Joan. *Worksteads: Living and Working in the Same Place.* New York: Dolphin, 1981.

Hoge, Cecil C. *Mail Order Know-How.* Berkeley, CA: Ten Speed Press, 1982.

Honigsberg, Peter J. *We Own It: Starting and Managing Co-ops, Collectives and Employee-Owned Ventures.* Laytonville, CA: Bell Springs Pub., 1982.

McCaslin, Barbara S., and Patricia P. McNamara. *Be Your Own Boss.* Englewood Cliffs, NJ: Prentice-Hall, 1980.

Whittlesey, Marietta. *Freelance Forever: Successful Self-Employment.* New York: Avon, 1982.

Technical Writing Careers

Dodds, Robert H. *Writing for Technical and Business Magazines.* Melborne, FL: Robert E. Krieger Pub. Co., 1982.

Sherman, Theodore A., and Simon Johnson. *Modern Technical Writing.* 4th ed. Englewood Cliffs, NJ: Prentice-Hall, 1983.

Travel Careers

Alston, Anna, and Angela Sharp. *Working in the Travel Business.* New York: State Mutual Books, 1982.

Hoosan, Christopher, and Nona Starr. *Travel Career Development.* Wellesley, MA: Institute of Certified Travel Agents, 1983.

Morton, Alexander C. *The Official 1982–1983 Guide to Travel Agent and Travel Careers.* New York: Arco, 1982.

Stevens, Laurence. *Guide to Starting and Operating a Successful Travel Agency.* (The Travel Management Library) Wheaton, IL: Merton House, 1984.

Word Processing Careers

Belkin, Gary. *How to Start and Run Your Own Word Processing Business.* (Small Business Series) New York: John Wiley & Sons, 1984.

Bergerud, Marly, and Jean Gonzalez. *Word Processing: Concepts and Careers.* 3rd ed. New York: John Wiley & Sons, 1984.

Foster, Timothy R. *Word Processing for Executives and Professionals.* New York: Van Nostrand Reinhold, 1983.

Glenn, Peggy. *Word Processing Profits at Home.* Huntington Beach, CA: Aames-Allen, 1983.

Index

Accountant, 77
Account executive, advertising, 38
ACTION Drug Prevention Program
  (ADPP), 73
ACTION programs, 72–73
Actuary, 77–78. *See also* Insurance
  sales
Administration, educational, 42–48
  in the community, 47–48
Administration, in nonprofit organiza-
  tions, 48–49
Administrative assistant, 78–79
Admissions officer
  college, 44–45
  private school, 48
Adult education, in training pro-
  grams, 9–14
Adult Educators Association, 11
Advertising field, 37–38, 53
Advertising sales, 53
Affirmative Action Officer, 78
Affirmative Action programs, 14
American Bankers Association, 80
American Society for Curriculum De-
  velopment, 82

American Society for Training and
  Development (ASTD), 13
Audio-visual specialist, 36–37
Automobile sales, 54–55

Banking careers, 79–80
Benefits, employee, 9
Benefits assistant, 27–28
Bookkeeper, 80
Brainstorming, 107–8
Burnout, teacher, *xii*
Business world, 1
  alternatives to, 7

Career counseling, 103
Career planning/placement counse-
  lors, 45
Certified Public Accountants
  (C.P.A.s), 77
CETA, 69
Chamber of Commerce, 61, 70, 112
Change, process of, 112–13
Changing Careers After Thirty-Five
  (Hiestand), 2

154

Chronicle of Higher Education, 43, 47

Civil service commission, state, 68, 69

COBOL (computer language), 16

Collection agent, 80

College administration, 42–47

College placement offices, services of, 92

Colleges, fundraising/development positions at, 82–83

Commissioner, in government, 70–71

Commitment, in job hunting, 113

Community colleges, 42, 46

Compensation assistant, 27–28

Compliance officer, government, 71

Computer consultant, 18–19

Computer education, 17·

Computer education publishing, 22–23

Computerese, 16

Computer industry, 15–25, 99

Computerland, 25

Computer languages, 16

Computer literacy, 16, 21

Computer operator, 24–25

Computer programming, 16–18

Computer programs
  debugging, 16–17
  writing, 16

Computer sales, 20–21

Computer technician, 25

Consultants, 14, 64
  computer, 18–19

Continuing education, 42, 46

Coordinator, 81

Copywriter, advertising, 37–38

Corporate liaison specialist, 46

Counselor, 81
  career, 45
  employment agency, 55–56

Courseware, computer, 22, 34

Cover letter, 92, 111
  samples, 96, 117

Curriculum developer, 81–82

Customer service representative, 82

Day care centers, teaching jobs in, 94

Dean of students, 45

Deming, W. Edwards, 89

Department of education, federal, 69

Departments of education, state, 69
  placement services, 92

Development, 82–83

Digital Equipment Corporation, 10

Discrimination, in hiring, 129, 131

Division of Employment Security (state), 69, 70

Editing, 33–34
  technical, 39

Education, adult, 9–14

Educational materials field, 34–35

Educational reform, *xiv*

Education Information Service, 97

Elderly, services for, 99–100, 102

Electronic News, 12

El-Hi Market 1984–89, The, 35

Employee programs. *See* Training

Employment agency counselor, 55–56

Employment and Training Administration, 70

Employment interviewer, 28–29

Employment services (state), jobs with, 69

Engineering aide, 83

Entrepreneurs, 57–66
  test for skills, 66

Entry-level jobs, 76–77

Equal Employment Opportunity Commission, 131

Equal Employment Opportunity (E.E.O) specialist, 78

ESANE, 63

Expediter, 89

Films, training, for industry, 37, 39

Financial aid personnel, 45

Ford Foundation, *xiv*

Ford Marketing Institute, 55

Foreign students, training and counseling of, 12

Foundation Directory, The, 95

Fundraising, 82–83

Gerontology, 102. *See also* Elderly

Government, jobs in, 67–75

Government/business joint programs, 69–70

Grant proposals, 94–95

Grants administrator, 46–47

Growth fields, 99–102
  actuary, 77–78
  computers, 15–25, 99
  health, 99–100
  market research, 86–87
  real estate sales, 51
  technical writing, 19–20, 38–39

Guidance counselors, college, 45

Handicapped services for, 100
Headhunters, 55
Health field, 99–100
Helping professions, 100–102
Hiestand, Dale I., 2
Human resources, training programs in, 9–14
Human resources director, 29

IBM, personal computers, 20–21
Individual's Guide to Grants, The, 95
Insurance sales, 52–53
Interests, identifying, 104
Interior decorator, 40–41
Interior designer, 40–41
Internship developer, 84
Interviewer, job, 120–21
    questions asked by, 123–27
    See also Job interview
Interviewing, for information, 103–4, 108–9. *See also* Job interview

Job analyst, 83
Job descriptions, 5, 6
    for Peace Corps, 75
Job developer, 71
Job fairs, high tech, 19
Job hunt
    length of, 7, 112
    steps in, 103–112
Job interview, 120–37
    "do's" and "don'ts," 118–20
    follow-up to, 129, 130 (sample letter)
    illegal questions in, 129, 131
    See also Interviewer, job
Job offer, 133–34, 137
Job titles, identifying, 105–6
Job Training Partnership Act, 69–70

Kinder-Care, 94

Language teaching
    abroad, 98
    in training programs, 10, 12
Legal assistant, 84–85
Legislative assistant, 71
Letter campaign, 95
Librarian, 85

Management by Objectives, 113
Manager, 85–86
Manufacturer's representative, 50–51
Market researcher, 86–87

Master of Business Administration (M.B.A), 6, 86
Mead, Margaret, 8
Medical assistant, 87
Medical field. *See* Health field
Micro-Computer Hardware and Software in the El-Hi Market 1983–87, 35
Middlesex Community College (Bedford, MA), 70
Minorities, 78, 86

National Association of Communicators, 35–36
National Center for Service Learning (NCSL), 73
National Commission on Excellence in Education, *xii*
Networking, 14, 104
Newsletter, in-house, 35–36
Newspaper ads, 55, 93
Nonprofit organizations, 48–49
Nontraditional careers, 87–88

Occupational Outlook Handbook, The, 108, 132
Office copying machine field, 25
Office manager, 88
Office of Volunteer Liaison (OVL), 73
"Overqualified," 5, 6–7

Paralegal, 84–85
Paramedic, 87
Partnership, in small business, 62
Part-time positions, 8, 33, 51, 64, 77, 100, 101
Peace Corps, 73–75
Personnel field, 26–30
    student, 44–46
Photography, 39–40
Physical/occupational therapist, 101
Placement offices, college, 92
Polaroid Corporation, 11
Portfolio, job hunt, creating a, 104
Private Industry Councils (PICs), 70
Private schools, administrative positions in, 48
Programming. *See* Computer programming
Project director/manager, 89
Proposal writer, 83
Public relations specialist, 31–33
Publishing, 33–34
    computer education, 22–23

textbook, 33
See also Writing
Purchasing agent, 88–89

Quality assurance field, 89–90

Radio and television specialists, 36
Real estate sales, 51–52
Recruiters
college, 44
employment agency, 55–56
personnel, 28
Re-entry teachers, 1–2
Resume, 92, 109–111
samples, 114–16
Retired Senior Volunteer Program
(RSVP), 73
Retirees, opportunities for, 3, 73
Risk, accepting, 113

Salaries
in business, 1
high, fields with, 7
Salary, negotiating, 131–37
Sales, 50–56
advertising, 53
automobile, 54–55
computer, 20–21
insurance, 52–53
in publishing, 33
real estate, 51–52
work schedule in, 8, 33
Sandy Pollack Associates, Inc., 58–59
Schools, visiting, 95
"School's Inn," (Lexington, MA), 62–
63
Self-employment, 57–66
as photographer, 40
in real estate sales, 52
Skills, identifying, 105
Small business(es)
failure rate of, 57–58
partnerships in, 62
steps in starting, 59–65
Small Business Administration (SBA),
61
Small Business Investment Company
(SBIC), 61
Social service agencies, fundraising
for, 82–83
Social worker, 102
Software, educational, 22, 34
Software applications, 16, 17
Speech/hearing specialist, 101–2

Stock broker, 53
Student personnel field, 44–46
Substitutes, 95–97
Systems analyst, 17

Teacher-placement agencies, private,
93
Teachers
reasons for seeking alternative careers, 1–4
re-entry, 1–2
Teachers' aide, 95–97
Teachers' associations
administrative positions in, 48, 49
placement services, 92–93
Teaching jobs, 91–98
abroad, 97–98
creating, 95
emergency openings, 93
Technical manuals, writing and editing, 19–20
Technical writing, 19–20, 38–39
training program in, 70
Telephone company, training program in, 12
Temporary employment agencies, 79
Tests
civil service, 68–69
vocational, 103
Textbook publishing, 33
Training field, 9–14
in banks, 79–80
in computer industry, 21–22
Training (retraining) programs, for
unemployed, 69–70
Travel agent, 53–54
Tutoring, 95–97

"Underqualified," 5, 7
United States Department of De-
fense, 97
United States Department of Educa-
tion, *xiv*
United States government, training
programs, 12–13
United States Office of Education, 69
Urban schools, *xiii*

Vacation time, 5
VISTA, 72
Vocational tests, 103
Volunteer positions, 72–75, 95
Volunteer programs, employment
with, 72–73

Wall Street Journal, 12
Women, 78, 86
  nontraditional careers for, 87–88
Word processing, 23–24
Working at home, 17, 57
Work schedules, 5, 8, 33, 57. *See also*
  Part-time positions
Workshops, running, 13–14
Writing
  in advertising field, 37–38

computer programs, 16
educational materials, 34–35
in-house newsletters, 35–36
of proposals, 83, 94–95
for teachers' publications, 94
technical, 19–20, 38–39
for television and radio, 36

Young Volunteers in ACTION (YVA),
  73

For Your Information

The Harvard Common Press is located in Boston, Massachusetts. We specialize in practical guides to small business, careers, travel, family matters, and cooking. We also have an imprint, *Gambit Books,* which includes illustrated children's books and literary titles. If you'd like to see a copy of our complete catalog, please write to us at: The Harvard Common Press, 535 Albany Street, Boston, Massachusetts 02118. Our books are available at bookstores or, if you'd like to order directly from us, please send a check for the cost of the book plus $2 postage and handling.

We have listed a few of our titles below that we thought might interest readers of this book.

The Job Search Companion
The Organizer for Job Seekers
By Ellen J. Wallach and Peter Arnold
$5.95 paperback, ISBN 0-916782-48-4
An easy-to-use, carry-everywhere organizer filled with proven techniques for finding the right job—all described in succinct and encouraging fashion. *The Job Search Companion* contains weekly calendars, contact data forms to refresh your memory, and graphic techniques for measuring your progress. *160 pages.*

A Young Person's Guide to Military Service
By Jeff Bradley
$8.95 paperback, ISBN 0-916782-32-8
$12.95 cloth, ISBN 0-916782-31-X

160   *For Your Information*

"A thorough, well-organized, information-packed examination of military careers." *(AL A Booklist)* This book provides a fresh and factual unbiased look at what the armed forces have to offer to-day's young person. *160 pages.*

The Teenager's Guide to the Best Summer Opportunities
By Jan W. Greenberg
$9.95 paperback, ISBN 0-916782-58-1
$14.95 cloth, ISBN 0-916782-59-X
A systematic, clear-headed guide to help teens get the most out of their summer, whether through jobs, learning, or adventure. Includes listings of programs, camps, job sources, exchanges, and national organizations for young people. *208 pages.*